THE
WILD
RIVER
AND THE
GREAT
DAM

THE CONSTRUCTION OF
HOOVER DAM
AND THE VANISHING
COLORADO
RIVER

THE WILD RIVER AND THE GREAT DAM

SIMON BOUGHTON

Christy Ottaviano Books

LITTLE, BROWN AND COMPANY
New York Boston

Interior design by Carla Weise.
Title page photo: Hoover Dam from the air, early 1940s.
Table of contents photo: High scalers and drillers, 1934.
Note photo: Black Canyon, 1934.

Interior art credits: Art deco frame © Tartila/Shutterstock.com;
Art deco border © LadadikArt/Shutterstock.com

Christy Ottaviano Books
Hachette Book Group
1290 Avenue of the Americas, New York, NY 10104
Visit us at LBYR.com

First Edition: March 2024

Christy Ottaviano Books is an imprint of Little, Brown and Company. The Christy
Ottaviano Books name and logo are trademarks of Hachette Book Group, Inc.

The publisher is not responsible for websites (or their content) that are not owned by
the publisher.

Little, Brown and Company books may be purchased in bulk for business, educational,
or promotional use. For information, please contact your local bookseller or the Hachette
Book Group Special Markets Department at special.markets@hbgusa.com.

Library of Congress Cataloging-in-Publication Data
Names: Boughton, Simon, author.
Title: The wild river and the great dam : the construction of Hoover Dam and the
vanishing Colorado River / Simon Boughton.
Description: First edition. | New York : Little, Brown and Company, 2024. | Includes
bibliographical references. | Audience: Ages 9–14 | Summary: "A nonfiction
exploration of the building of the Hoover Dam, revealing the causes, effects,
and lasting legacies of one of America's most recognizable and misrepresented
landmarks." —Provided by publisher.
Identifiers: LCCN 2023004800 | ISBN 9780316380744 (hardcover) | ISBN
9780316380959 (ebook)
Subjects: LCSH: Hoover Dam (Ariz. And Nev.)—Juvenile literature. | Colorado River
Watershed (Colo.-Mexico)—Environmental conditions—Juvenile literature.
Classification: LCC TC557.5.H6 B68 2024 | DDC 627/.820979159—dc23/
eng/20230202
LC record available at https://lccn.loc.gov/2023004800

ISBNs: 978-0-316-38074-4 (hardcover), 978-0-316-38095-9 (ebook)

Printed in Indiana, USA

LSC-C

Printing 2, 2024

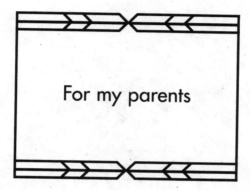

For my parents

CONTENTS

THE NAME OF THE DAM

IN THIS BOOK, HOOVER DAM IS REFERRED TO BY ITS FAMILIAR MODERN name. But in the 1930s and '40s, it was most often called Boulder Dam, after Boulder Canyon on the Colorado River, where the United States government had planned to build it. As it turned out, the dam was located in Black Canyon, twenty miles downriver, but the act of Congress that authorized its construction was called the Boulder Canyon Project Act, and Boulder Dam remained its official name.

Then when construction started, the secretary of the interior decided that the dam would be named for his boss, President Herbert Hoover. Hoover wasn't a popular president, and the name wasn't popular either: Kids in nearby Boulder City reversed street signs pointing to "Hoover Dam" so that they pointed instead to the town garbage dump. After President Franklin Roosevelt took office in 1933, the new administration changed the name back to Boulder Dam. It remained Boulder Dam until 1947, when Congress gave it the name by which it is known today.

"The father of all the dams": Hoover Dam in 1941, five years after it was completed, in a picture taken by the celebrated landscape photographer Ansel Adams.

No other single piece of man's
handiwork in this vast wilderness
hinterland has epitomized so
well during its construction
all the strange and complex
ramifications of our
American Way.

—FRANK WATERS, *THE COLORADO*

Hoover Dam rises in the desert in February 1935. The biggest structure built in the United States at the time, it provided work for more than twenty thousand men during the worst years of the Great Depression, tamed the fastest-flowing, muddiest, most temperamental major river in the country, and transformed the landscape and economies of the Southwest.

"IT IS AS IF OUR COUNTRY SUDDENLY HAD A NEW STATE ADDED TO IT"

JOE KINE DANGLED FROM A ROPE FIVE HUNDRED FEET ABOVE THE COLOrado River. His seat was a narrow wooden board, like a child's swing. In front of him was a sheer rock wall, and in his hands was the latest compressed-air-powered jackhammer. Leaning back in his seat with the jackhammer in between his boots, and nothing but empty air below, Joe hammered away at loose and uneven rock. He had a pry bar made of duralumin alloy to help break off small pieces. For bigger outcrops, there were explosives: He drilled a hole in the rock, inserted a charge, and retreated a safe distance as it was set off.

Joe was a high scaler. His job was to help smooth and shape the cliff face for a massive dam being built across the Colorado River. Hoover Dam would be the biggest structure in the United States and the biggest dam in the world: a curving wall of concrete a quarter of a mile across, almost two-thirds as tall as the Empire State Building (just opened in New York City), and as thick at its base as a battleship was long. Its purpose was to stop the floods and droughts that plagued the southwestern United States: It would control the fastest-flowing, muddiest, most unpredictable major river in the country, and create a vast reservoir to store and supply water to the region's farms, cities, and industry. When it was full, the reservoir would hold as much water as flowed down the Colorado River in two years and weigh so much that it deflected the earth's crust and caused hundreds of small earthquakes.

Joe worked eight hours a day, seven days a week. The percussive clack-clack-clack of the jackhammers, the roar of trucks and machinery on the construction site far below, and from time to time the blast of an explosion filled the canyon with noise. From above, a hard desert sun scorched everything, making tools too hot to pick up without gloves. Handling a forty-five-pound jackhammer while swinging from a rope left Joe's neck and shoulders aching and his hands blistered and calloused. Air hoses, water bags, and other equipment hung scattered across the rock face, waiting to trip up a careless high scaler. Falling rock and tools dropped by other workers could become deadly missiles. To protect themselves, some high scalers wore homemade "hard-boiled hats": a pair of canvas baseball hats placed one atop the other, then soaked in pine tar or glue and allowed to harden.

High scalers were paid $5.60 per day, more than a dollar a day more than most workers on the ground below. It was 1932, the middle of the Great Depression, and jobs were scarce—but high scaling wasn't for everyone. "A lot of these guys were pretty hungry," remembered dam worker Tommy Nelson. "Some of them thought they were high scalers… and they'd come down on the job on the bus, and when they looked up where they had to work, why, they said, 'It's too high for me.' They weren't that hungry." Another man said, "They hired anybody that didn't have enough brains to be scared."

High scaler at Hoover Dam.

High scaling was dangerous and difficult, and if Joe slipped and fell, the work going on around him would barely pause. One day Tommy Nelson was directing traffic on the ground and made the mistake of stopping the trucks when a high scaler fell, and a foreman chewed him out: "He said, 'Get those trucks moving.' I said, 'There's a man killed over here.' 'Well, he won't hurt anybody, get 'em going.'"

But for those who could stand the height, high scaling wasn't too bad a job: As far as Joe was concerned, "it wasn't any worse than anything else." And along with the high wages it had an advantage over many other jobs on the site. "You were sitting down all the time," Joe said. "It was a sitting-down job."

Below the high scalers, four enormous tunnels were being driven through the canyon walls alongside the river. Marion Allen was a nipper, a driller's assistant, working on the lowest level of a drilling rig called a jumbo. Marion's job was to hand drill bits and other equipment up to a man working above him. Water and rock dust rained down on him and the other men on the lower levels of the jumbo from the drills above. "The miners under there, I think, was the ones they [the foremen] didn't like, because all the water and everything came down on you." But Marion added, "It was a good, safe place....If something caved in, it might get the ones above you, but not you."

All the same, there were plenty of ways for miners to get hurt—tunneling, not high scaling, was the most dangerous work building the dam. Miners used long wooden rods to tap explosive charges into place in boreholes drilled into the rock face; if the charge got stuck and the miner tapped too hard, the explosives could detonate, sending a deadly blast of rock back into the tunnel. Sometimes one charge among the dozens placed in the holes failed to go off and lay like an unexploded bomb among the rubble from a blast, where a strike from a tool or a power shovel could accidentally detonate it.

Miners checked the tunnels for faults in the rock, and after each blast, but cave-ins could happen without warning. As they were starting

Miners at work on a drilling jumbo.

their shift one evening, Marion and the other members of his crew were teasing a new miner about his clean white shirt. A few minutes later, the young miner was dead, killed by a sudden collapse in the tunnel roof. It felt like an explosion, and Marion remembered desperately trying to pry slabs of rock off the man. "All I could see of him was one foot."

Staying safe in the thick, dark atmosphere in the tunnels among high-powered machinery, explosives, and racing trucks required care and luck. More than once Marion's luck almost ran out. One night at the end of his shift a foreman sent him back into the tunnel to deliver a message. "I had gone quite a way when I had a funny feeling something was wrong. Then I realized it was too quiet." Marion had made a mistake and walked into the wrong tunnel as a blast was about to be fired. He started to run, but it was too late. The blast hurled him down the tunnel and flat on his face. Dazed but too embarrassed to tell anyone what happened, he got up and delivered the message, but the explosion left him with a headache that lasted days. "The next shift when I went on the job my head felt as big as a barrel," he said. The blast had ruptured both his eardrums—although he didn't find that out until years later. At the time, he was examined at the construction company hospital and allowed to go back to work. "They just figured if I could hear, I was alright."

Instead of working hundreds of feet up the canyon walls like Joe or in the dark underground like Marion, Curley Francis spent his shifts driving a truck. "The reason I liked it so well was that we traveled over the job quite a bit," he explained. "There was a lot of interesting things that I could see going on." Trucks and heavy machines were everywhere, and at one time or another Curley operated most of them. Running a power shovel was called mucking. Clearing rock and dirt with one of the diesel-powered Caterpillar bulldozers was mucking out, and the drivers were known as cat skinners, after the name of the machine's manufacturer. Debris was loaded into muck trucks—dump trucks—to be removed. Like many of the machines being used to build the dam, dump trucks were new technology, developed in the 1920s. The 250-horsepower Macks working on the site were the newest and biggest in the world; they could carry up to sixteen cubic yards of muck. The trucks pounded up steep, twisty canyon roadways to drop their loads at dump sites out of the way of construction, or dumped them into train cars to be hauled away.

The machines never stopped. At the beginning of a shift, truck drivers took the first truck they could find and kept moving. "Those trucks never turned their ignition off unless they were broke down....They would change shifts right on the run," remembered one dam worker. To save time, the trucks often didn't turn around after dumping their loads, instead traveling one way in reverse. The driver stood facing backward with one foot on the gas, peering over the truck bed to see where he was going, and turned around only when it was time to hit the brakes. It took skill, and there was no time to learn on the job: A foreman "could tell within an hour or so whether you were a truck driver," said Curley, and "if you wasn't, you weren't"—and you were quickly reassigned to another job, or sent home.

Dump trucks reversing down a construction road, with their drivers facing backward.

Curley, Marion, and Joe were three of the more than twenty thousand men who built Hoover Dam. They came from every state in the country. Some were experienced construction workers who moved from project to project. Many were not: men who had lost jobs in the Depression and had come to the damsite desperate to find any sort of work.

Together with the massive dam, they built two power generation plants, overflow channels called spillways, four intake towers to draw water from the reservoir—each four hundred feet tall, the height of a thirty-story skyscraper—and a vast network of tunnels, pipes, gates, and valves. They poured more concrete than the US government had used in all its previous dam-building projects combined. The four main water tunnels—fifty feet in diameter, totaling three miles in length—were the largest ever dug through solid rock. Even the smaller details were enormous: The dam's water pipes, for example, required eighty-eight million pounds of steel and were assembled in sections each weighing as much as a railroad locomotive.

Not only was the dam huge but the construction site was in a remote canyon in the desert, where summer temperatures reached well over 100 degrees. Black Canyon, on the border between Nevada and Arizona 250 miles downriver from the Grand Canyon, was over nine hundred feet deep. It was narrow, with few places for workers to land and set up equipment, and the Colorado River could change from a sluggish stream to a dangerous torrent in a matter of hours. The nearest town, and the nearest railroad and paved road, was Las Vegas, thirty miles away. At that time, Las Vegas was a small railroad town with a population of just five thousand people. Its main street, Fremont, had only been paved in 1925. Materials, machines, and men had to be transported first to Las Vegas, and then across the desert to the river. There was no housing, only limited access to water, and no other facilities for the thousands of workers who would come with their families to build the dam.

Dynamite blasts echoed in Black Canyon in May 1931, beginning construction. Five years later and two years ahead of schedule, in October 1936, hydroelectric generators at Hoover Dam were switched on and electricity made there lit up streets in Los Angeles, three hundred miles away.

What made the completion of such a vast, complicated, and daring construction project in just five years possible?

First was technology: Hoover Dam could not have been built twenty years earlier, before the invention and development of motorized

1922: Looking upstream through Black Canyon. Hoover Dam would rise roughly in the middle of the photo, near the small outcrop on the right at river level.

shovels, earthmovers and dump trucks, jackhammers, and other power equipment. "This is a job for machines and all of these machines will be power driven," the engineer in charge of building Hoover Dam told the press. Second was ingenuity: of the civil engineers who imagined, designed, and planned the dam and of the construction engineers who put those machines to work building something that had never been built before.

Third was the labor of those thousands of men. They worked twenty-four hours a day in three shifts, seven days a week, with just four days off a year (at Christmas and Fourth of July), for a total of more than thirty-one million man-hours. Most worked for $5 a day or less—enough for a family to live on in the 1930s, but only just. The work was difficult and dangerous, and conditions were harsh: Building the dam so fast was possible because the safety and welfare of those men was sometimes overlooked, and when they were hurt or sick, or refused to work due to poor conditions, thousands of others were waiting to take their place. More than a hundred men lost their lives building Hoover Dam, and many more were injured. Attempts by the workers to strike for better conditions were quickly broken.

Finally, Hoover Dam was possible because those who built it had no doubt that it was the right thing to do. The story of the dam reaches back to the 1850s, when white European Americans began arriving in the Colorado River Valley and the surrounding desert: first miners and small farmers, then investors and industrial farmers, and then the United States government, with a vision of harnessing the Colorado to support the population and the economy of an entire region stretching from Arizona to the Pacific Ocean. To them, water was wasted if it flowed down the river and reached the sea instead of being put to use by people. Building the dam would be "as if our country suddenly had a new State added to it," in the words of Ray Lyman Wilbur, who was the US secretary of the interior when construction began. "A new and wider use of this controlled water will care for millions of people and create billions of wealth."

Secretary Wilbur's words proved true—for a time. When it was finished, the great dam was celebrated as a triumph. It provided water for farming, industry, drinking, and bathing; reservoirs for boating and recreation; cheap electricity for homes and factories; and security from droughts and floods. Its success led the way for dozens more dams and water management systems to be built on the Colorado River. They fueled the economies and supported the growing populations of Los Angeles, Las Vegas, Phoenix, and the other cities of the desert.

But by the end of the twentieth century, the world that Hoover Dam helped create threatened to overwhelm it. The thirsty, expanding farms and cities around the Colorado drew more and more water out of the river, while years of drought put less in. Today, the vast reservoir behind Hoover Dam is only about a third full. It is not certain that it will ever reach its full capacity again or that the world that the dam builders imagined will return.

Yet it's difficult to think of the West without the dam and the reservoir, and the water they provide. Almost a hundred years after they were built, they seem to be a permanent part of the desert landscape, and forty million people depend on the Colorado River for some part of their water or power needs.

And it's hard to imagine the wild, muddy river that once flowed in Black Canyon, or the army of men who once worked there. But for five years they and their machines filled the canyon with deafening noise and constant activity, and they left behind a river and a land forever changed.

This is the story of the men, the dam, and the river. It begins thirty years before work started in Black Canyon and three hundred miles to the south, in the driest place in the country, with the biggest flood in United States history.

A man stands on a washed-out section of railroad track on the edge of the Salton Sea in August 1906. Fed by the flooding Colorado River, what had been dry desert became a lake covering more than 450 square miles that was rising by seven inches a day. Stopping the flood would take two years and lead the US government to look for a way to tame the wild river once and for all.

ONE

THE WILD COLORADO

*"The Colorado don't submit
till it has to"*

FEBRUARY 2, 1905. ABOUT FIVE MILES WEST OF YUMA, ARIZONA, ON THE US-Mexican border, the Colorado River had found a weakness in the embankments—or levees—that kept it on its course to the ocean in the Gulf of California. The weakness had been created by people: Engineers working for the California Development Company had cut an opening in the river's western levee to divert water to irrigate farms in California's Imperial Valley. That day, the river had been swollen by a sudden winter flood, and now it was gnawing at the edges of the opening and spilling into the surrounding land. At first, the flood subsided and the level of the river fell, but two weeks later the river flooded again, followed by a third flood a week after that. Engineers tried to close the opening with sandbags and brush, but these were washed away when another flood struck in March. The opening in the levee grew. After yet another flood, in the middle of April, it was more than 150 feet wide. A torrent of water was pouring through it toward the Imperial Valley—and the worst of the Colorado River's yearly cycle of floods was still to come.

The Colorado is usually lowest in winter and highest during early summer, when snow melts in the Rocky Mountains to the north and fills the river. When the California Development Company engineers made the opening in the riverbank the previous September, they had planned to close it again before the summer flood season. They had not anticipated the possibility of flooding in winter: Their records showed the Colorado had flooded only three times during winter, and never more than once in the same year. "I doubt as to whether anyone should be accused of negligence or carelessness in failing to foresee what had never happened before," the company's chief engineer, Charles Rockwood, wrote later. But for Rockwood, "never" meant only twenty-seven years; that's as far back as the records went. Unfortunately, they told only a tiny fraction of the Colorado River's long and unpredictable story.

Making matters worse for the California Development Company, the Imperial "Valley" was not in fact a valley, but part of a giant bowl that lay below the level of the river; much of it was even below sea level. When the Colorado burst its banks, there was nowhere for the water to go except down into the bottom of the bowl, to an area called the Salton Sink, where it began to form a lake. This had happened naturally in the past: Five hundred years earlier, the Colorado River had fed a hundred-mile-long lake in the same place, until the river changed course to the south and the lake dried up. Now the mistake made by the development company's engineers threatened the same thing. If the opening in the levees continued to grow, the Colorado could change course permanently, turning the area into a vast inland lake once more.

But for now, the river was still flowing south on its familiar path to the ocean. The flooding and the growing lake, called the Salton Sea, were still far from the Imperial Valley's towns and farms. When a US government engineer visited the area in April, he thought the situation was "not serious, but sufficiently alarming to require some attention."

That would soon change. During the summer of 1905, as the annual floods raised the level of the river, sheets of water crept toward the border towns of Calexico and Mexicali, fifty miles to the west, washing out bridges and leaving people stranded on rooftops. In early fall, a dam was built to try to direct the Colorado around the break in the levee. It was destroyed in late November, when the Colorado was struck by its biggest flood in more than fifteen years. The river rose ten feet in just ten hours, and when it subsided, the dam was in splinters and the break had grown to more than six hundred feet wide. The Colorado River was now flowing west through the opening toward the Imperial Valley, instead of south toward the ocean. It had changed course.

Two more attempts to control the river and close the break began that winter. Work went on around the clock, but neither was finished by spring, when the river started to rise again. By June 1906, more than two billion gallons of water an hour were pouring through the opening, which was now half a mile wide. On June 30, the town of Mexicali was flooded. "The river chewed into Mexicali with relentless fury, carrying away practically the entire town….Nearly all the houses in Mexicali being built of adobe or brick could not be moved so fell into the stream and were a total loss," reported the *Imperial Valley Press*. North of the border, in neighboring Calexico, the California Development Company, whose engineers had caused the flood, was forced out of its headquarters by the rising waters.

Flooding near Calexico, June 1906.

Rivers of floodwater formed cutbacks in the earth: places where the fast-moving water eroded a gorge and a waterfall formed at its upstream end. As the water plunged over the falls, it "cut back" through the soft soil, creating a cataract that moved upriver while people watched. The biggest and most terrifying were on the New River, which had once been a dry channel and was now carrying much of the floodwater north to the Salton Sea. In some places, the cutback chewed its way upstream as much as a mile a day and left behind a gorge eighty feet deep and a thousand feet across. Clouds of dust hung in the air overhead, and the distant, dreadful roar of the water could be heard from the region's towns and farms. And at the end of the New River, the Salton Sea continued to grow: By the summer of 1906 it covered an area of 450 square miles and was rising by seven inches a day. The lake was growing so fast that some people refused to believe that the Colorado River could be the cause and suggested instead that the Pacific Ocean had somehow broken through a crack in the earth and was filling it from below.

Cutback on the New River, June 1906: Water erodes a gorge in the soft soil, creating a waterfall almost thirty feet high.

People dynamited the cutbacks to try and change their course. Buildings were dismantled and railroad tracks were moved away from the floodwaters. Near the town of Brawley, farmers cut off by the flood set up a cable across the New River, and for almost a year they sent their crops to market in a cage—until they were forced to evacuate with their possessions the same way. But they believed that the situation would be brought under control. "The Colorado river will be sent back where it belongs and an end put to its bad actions in discharging into Salton Sea.... The river will be shut out," wrote the *Press* at the height of the 1906 flood. "Before this is accomplished, however, there will be quite a fight, for the Colorado don't submit till it has to."

The fight would take another six months and use almost all the resources of the Southern Pacific Railroad. The California Development Company had run out of money, and the Southern Pacific had stepped in, first with a loan, and then to take charge. In September, crews began building jetties from each side of the break in the Colorado's bank. The jetties were joined by a railroad trestle, and then locomotives began pulling sideways-dumping railroad cars called battleships onto the trestle, where they poured loads of rock into the water. As the barrier rose, the spaces between the rocks were filled with clay and gravel. For almost a month, more than three hundred battleships shuttled back and forth, dumping load after load of rock. By early October the opening was almost closed and the flood had slowed to a trickle.

But the fight wasn't over. To maintain a supply of irrigation water to the Imperial Valley's farms, a new channel had been opened nearby with a wooden headgate, which could be raised and lowered to control the

A side-dumping train car, or battleship, drops a load of rock into the break in the levee.

flow of water from the Colorado into the irrigation canals. The gate was badly constructed, and water ate away at its foundation. On the afternoon of October 11 it collapsed. It washed out a railroad trestle and a train— and the Colorado began flooding into the surrounding land once more.

To stop the flood, crews used the same method they used to close the original gap, dumping rock into the water from the battleships and damming the channel at the site of the destroyed headgate. No sooner had they finished than the river burst through its banks a third time, this time on the other side of the original break. The trains and the work crews turned around and began extending the levee in that direction. Rock was hauled from as far as four hundred miles away, and for three weeks in January almost every railroad car the Southern Pacific owned was occupied with the flood—freight unloaded from ships in the port of Los Angeles sat on the docks because no trains were available to move it. The trestle over the break was swept away and had to be rebuilt three times. It took roughly three thousand carloads of rock, but on February 10, 1907, the break was closed—and this time, the levee held. The Colorado River had been put back in its course and the flood, which had lasted two years and left behind the biggest lake in California, was over.

Too Thick to Drink and Too Thin to Plow

Why did the Southern Pacific spend so much money and effort to stop a flood in a desert? The answer lay in the ground.

The Colorado River was loaded with mud. It carried a greater concentration of dirt and rock particles—called silt—than almost any river in the world. The amount of this mud, around 275 million tons a year, was enough to fill a football stadium once a week. It gave the river its distinctive color and its name: the Spanish word "colorado" means "reddish in color." It also gave it a thick, soupy consistency. People said the Colorado was too thick to drink and too thin to plow.

The river got its dirt from the deserts of Utah and Arizona and its power from the mountains of Colorado and Wyoming. It began high in the Rocky Mountains, where it was fed by hundreds of fast-flowing smaller streams and rivers, and fell almost thirteen thousand feet before it reached the ocean. When the snow in the mountains melted, it filled the river with water and energy. "Ten million cascade brooks unite to form ten thousand torrent creeks; ten thousand torrent creeks unite to form a hundred rivers beset with cataracts; a hundred roaring rivers unite to form the Colorado, which rolls a mad, turbid stream into the Gulf of California," wrote one of the first white people to travel the river, John Wesley Powell, thirty years before the Imperial Valley flood.

Where it left the mountains behind and flowed south and west across the desert, the "mad, turbid stream" had carved deep canyons, one after the other, in the landscape—including the biggest canyon on earth, the Grand Canyon. The canyons were formed over millions of years as the powerful river slowly cut down through the soft rock. That rock went south, pulverized and carried away by the Colorado in the form of silt. But lower down, toward the ocean, the river flattened out and slowed down, and as it slowed it dropped the silt and left it behind. Gradually, the silt built up, leaving a layer of soil that stretched from the Gulf of California to the Salton Sea. In some places, this soil was many hundreds of feet deep. The rock that once filled the Grand Canyon and its neighbors became the earth in the Imperial Valley.

Although this river-borne dirt had created a deep layer of fertile soil, few things grew there naturally because of the lack of rain. The southwestern United States is a desert. Large parts of Utah, Arizona, Nevada, and Southern California receive less than ten inches of rain a year, and the Colorado Desert, which stretches west from the Colorado

River across southeastern California, receives less than five inches—the driest place in the United States.

But although there was no rain, there was water: the Colorado River. If the river could be diverted to irrigate the soil, fruits and vegetables and other sun-loving crops could be grown in the desert. In fact, they could be grown there better than almost anywhere: With plentiful, fertile soil, year-round sunshine, and no frost, two or even three crops a year could be produced.

In 1896, speculators formed the California Development Company to build an irrigation system and sell water to the white European American settlers they hoped would come to the desert. To attract them, they set up a separate company to promote settlement and develop land for farming. They gave the terrible-sounding "Colorado Desert" a new name, the Imperial Valley, and called the company the Imperial Land Company. For $1.25 an acre, settlers could buy plots of land from the federal government; the speculators would make money by requiring farmers to buy shares in the water company and selling them the water.

The first white farmers arrived in the Imperial Valley at the beginning of 1901—but they didn't find any water. It wasn't until May that year that a channel was opened from the Colorado and water was delivered to the Imperial Valley. Meanwhile, the newcomers worked for the water company digging canals and ditches in the desert heat. But once the water started to flow, the white population of the valley grew quickly. By January 1903, there were two thousand newcomers; a year later, there were about seven thousand, and a year after that, by January 1905, the population had doubled again, to almost fourteen thousand. There were

GOVERNMENT LANDS
WITH CHEAP WATER
IN THE
IMPERIAL SETTLEMENT

**Do you want a ranch in Southern California?
A ranch of first class soil at the government
price of $1.25 per acre?
With a right at small cost to all the irrigation water that can be used?
At an annual expense for water lower than ever
before offered on the pacific coast?**

If so, the following information will interest you.

The Colorado River furnishes the most abundant supply of water for irrigation purposes to be found west of the Rocky Mountains. Its greatest supply is furnished during the month of June, when it is needed the most, and the least supply during December, when it is needed the least—the river being about nine feet higher in June than in December.

The river carries enough water to irrigate 8,000,000 acres of land, hence the supply can never be cut short by dry seasons.

The Colorado Delta, located in Riverside and San Diego counties in Southern California and extending down into Lower California, comprises about 1,000,000 acres of level, irrigable land that has been made during the past ages by alluvial deposits carried down by the waters of the Colorado River.

The waters of this river carry more fertilizers than is carried by the waters of any other river in world, not excepting ever the Nile.

The soil of this Delta is therefore as fertile as soil can be, and when it is cultivated and irrigated by water from this source of supply, it must continue to remain fertile, as each season's irrigation will deposit on each acre irrigated more than $10 worth of commercial fertilizers aeposited by the water without extra expense.

An extensive irrigation system is now being constructed to reclaim this large tract of country. The main canal will be enlarged and the main branch canals extended to meet the demand for water as the irrigated area is enlarged.

The land to be reclaimed is located in San Diego county, east of the New River, and embraces 500,000 acres of level, fertile land, free from alkali, with sufficient slope to be easily irrigated. It is all Government land and can be taken up under the desert land law or the homestead law. 320 acres can be taken up by each person under the desert land law, and residence on the land is not required. This liberal law is liable to be repealed or unfavorably modified soon.

This tract will be irrigated by mutual water companies, designated as Imperial Water Company No. 1, No. 2, No. 3, etc., which companies are formed to distribute water to stockholders only, at cost.

The Imperial Land Company sells this water stock to the landowners—one share to each acre. The price is now only $11.25 per share.

A branch railroad tapping the Imperial Settlement connecting with the Southern Pacific, is on the program

This country is suited to the production of alfalfa and other farm products, and the fattening of cattle, a line of business that can never be overdone.

It is also believed that this will become a great early fruit country.

Water will be ready for use for fall and winter crops.

For circular matter and full information, address

IMPERIAL LAND CO.

S. W. FERGUSSON, General Manager.   **IMPERIAL, VIA FLOWINGWELL, CAL.**

An advertisement by the Imperial Land Company promoting settlement in the Imperial Valley, published in the *Imperial Press* in 1901.

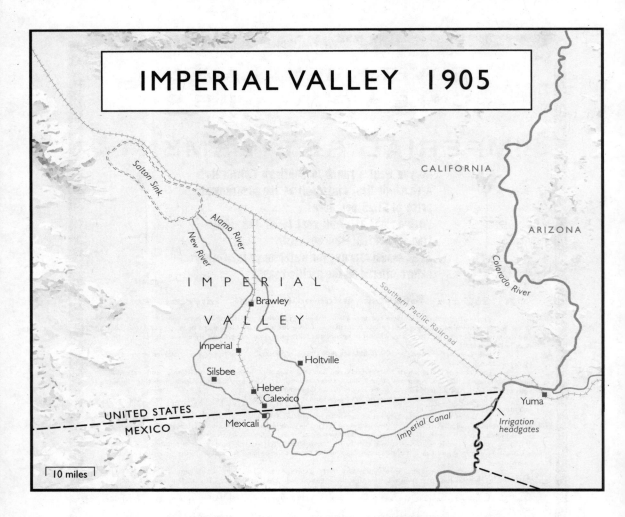

half a dozen towns, a newspaper, and a railroad. Almost eight hundred miles of irrigation canals watered 120,000 acres of land, producing barley, alfalfa, fruits, vegetables, and grazing for cattle and other livestock.

But as the water company and the farmers quickly discovered, the Colorado River was unreliable, unmanageable, and dangerous. The irrigation system was poorly designed and became clogged with silt from the river, and the California Development Company didn't have the resources to maintain it. Farmers complained that the water they had been promised didn't arrive.

Then came the floods. When the Southern Pacific stepped in, it was to stop thousands of acres of farmland from disappearing under a vast lake. But saving the Imperial Valley came at a high cost. Diverting the Colorado River had bankrupted the California Development Company. Putting it back where it belonged when things went wrong cost the Southern Pacific Railroad more than $3 million (about $98 million in 2023 dollars). Keeping the river there—and keeping it under control— was too big a task for local farmers or for a railroad company. It was a task for the United States government.

"The Lord left that damsite there"

In January 1921, the US government sent a party of surveyors to Nevada to look for a place to build a dam on the Colorado. They first set up camp near Boulder Canyon, forty miles east of Las Vegas, and began drilling into the river bottom to test the depth and stability of the bedrock below. The drilling barges were anchored to the canyon walls with steel cables, but swirling currents and flood surges could upset the boats and send men and equipment tumbling into the water. Floods could also bring tree-size driftwood and sometimes even animal carcasses down the river, propelling them like torpedoes at the anchored boats. "That Colorado River was not a tame river," said the crew chief, Walker Young. "That river at that time would rise six inches in an hour." While the drillers worked on the river, other teams climbed the sheer rock walls of the canyon to measure their exact shape and dimensions.

When they couldn't
reach the measur-
ing points from the
ground, they low-
ered themselves on
ropes from the cliff
tops.

The purpose of
a dam would be to
control the river, ab-
sorbing the unpre-
dictable floods and
surges that threat-
ened the farms and
towns downstream,
and to store water
that could be used to
irrigate those farms
and provide those

A drilling barge anchored on the Colorado River during surveying, 1922.

towns with a steady supply of drinking water and power. But the government's vision had grown since the Imperial Valley flood: Building a
dam on the Colorado was part of a plan to provide flood control and supply water not just to the Imperial Valley but across the desert Southwest,
in Arizona, Nevada, and California—"a broad comprehensive scheme
of development for all the irrigable land upon the Colorado River...so
that none of the water of this great river which can be put to beneficial

use will be allowed to go to waste," said President Theodore Roosevelt in 1907.

Planning and building the dam was the job of a government agency called the Bureau of Reclamation. The white European Americans who colonized the western United States in the second half of the nineteenth century found that almost all the western half of the country was dry, or arid, and that water was a scarce and precious resource. Without water, land couldn't be farmed, and towns and cities couldn't grow. The bureau's mission was to "reclaim" arid land by building dams and irrigation systems. It was created in 1902, and by the time Walker Young began surveying in Boulder Canyon, it had already built almost a hundred dams to store and divert water for irrigation and other uses, from Wyoming and Washington in the north to Arizona and Southern California in the south. But none of them were as big or as ambitious as the dam the bureau proposed to build in the Nevada desert.

The government estimated that there were a million acres or more that could be irrigated along the lower part of the Colorado River, which would require a reservoir that could store more than six million acre-feet of water. (One acre-foot is the amount of water that covers one acre of land to a depth of one foot, or about 326,000 gallons.) So the dam had to be built in a place where there was space for a giant reservoir. And by stopping the river, the dam would also cause it to drop the silt that plagued irrigation canals, so the reservoir would need to be big enough not just to store the water but to collect the silt, too.

The best site for a dam would be a narrow, deep canyon: A narrow dam would require less concrete and wouldn't cost as much to build. The rock on which the dam was built had to be solid, without faults or the chance that an earthquake could cause it to collapse. And the site had to be within three hundred miles of Los Angeles. To pay for itself, the project would include a power plant that used the water released from the reservoir to spin turbines and generate electricity, which the government would sell to Los Angeles and other cities in the Southwest. At that time, three hundred miles was as far as electricity could be carried over transmission wires.

Walker Young and his crew of around fifty men spent the spring and fall carefully mapping Boulder Canyon. (They took off two months in the summer, when the temperature approached 120 degrees Fahrenheit and their instruments couldn't take accurate measurements in the heat.) For company they had small wild donkeys called burros, which tried to steal their food: "They would eat most anything that anybody would eat, and a lot of things that most of us shouldn't eat," Young said. Occasionally, drunk miners passed through the surveying camp on their way to the river from a mine in the desert nearby. Walker Young's daughter remembered that her mother kept a gun under her pillow in their tent, "just in case."

But as it turned out, the bedrock beneath Boulder Canyon was fractured and cut by faults, and where the rock was stable the canyon was so narrow that the river swept its sides, which would make it hard to reach with construction equipment. In search of a better place for a dam, Young moved his crew down the river to Black Canyon, twenty miles to the south. There they found a site where a tall dam could be built, with easier access for men and machines—and Black Canyon was closer to the railroad in Las Vegas, so the men and machines wouldn't have to travel as far to reach the construction site. The bedrock was stable, and there was less silt and gravel in the bottom of the river, meaning it would be easier to excavate the foundation for a dam. Finally, building a dam in Black Canyon would create a bigger reservoir than building one farther north in Boulder Canyon.

The reservoir would submerge dozens and possibly hundreds of sites used over centuries by Indigenous people, as well as some settled more recently by European American farmers, but the government paid little attention to that. White farmers would be compensated, Indigenous people mostly disregarded. There were almost no systematic archaeological surveys to catalog or preserve what would be lost from the past, or environmental impact studies to determine what in the future might happen to the natural world of the river. The Bureau of Reclamation's goal was to dam the river and manage the water in it, and Young and his team had found the place to do it.

"The Lord left that damsite there," he said. "It was only up to man to discover it and use it."

"People were standing on the street selling apples"

Before a dam could be built, the seven states along the Colorado River had to agree on how to share the water that would be stored in the reservoir, and the United States Congress had to agree to provide the money for construction. Neither happened quickly.

Representatives from the states met in Washington in January 1922. There had never been a negotiated agreement among more than three US states at once, and here there were seven—and they had different ideas about what was fair. Most of the water in the river came from melting snow in the mountains in the states in the north: Colorado and Wyoming. Those states thought that they should get to keep it. But most of the water was *used* to irrigate farms in the desert states in the south: Arizona and especially California. Those states thought that since they were putting the water to use, they should get the bigger share. To make things more complicated, there were two different sets of laws that could be used to decide who "owned" the water in a river. The first, called riparian law, said that the water belonged to the owner of the land alongside the river. The second, called prior appropriation, said the water belonged to whoever first put it to "beneficial use"—even if they were far from the river. In the western United States, where water was scarce and farmers and miners diverted it away from rivers through irrigation canals and sluices, it was this principle of prior appropriation that came to govern how water was managed.

It took almost a year for the states to agree, and when they did, they did not agree about much. In November 1922, they signed the Colorado River Compact. Together with the water use agreements that followed, the compact became known as the Law of the River. It divided the area drained by the Colorado into two parts, the upper basin and the lower basin, and gave each basin the right to use—or "develop"—half the water estimated to flow down the Colorado in a year. But the compact left it up to the states in each basin to agree among themselves how to divide their share, and arguments between them would continue long after Hoover Dam was finished. The negotiations did not include Mexico, although Mexican territory formed part of the Colorado River Basin. Nor did they include Indigenous nations, who had reservation land in all seven states, and the compact was silent about their rights to water from the river.

Meanwhile, in April 1922, congressmen from California introduced a bill to provide money to build the dam—but it failed to pass. It was opposed by private power utility companies, which objected to the federal government making and selling electricity in competition with them; by congressmen from southern states, who objected to the federal government funding a project that would support farmers in the west; and by cautious congressmen who objected to the huge expense. It was estimated that the project would cost as much as $130 million—more than half the annual federal budget for public works.

But the population and political power of the southwestern states—especially California—were growing fast. The bill was introduced three more times and finally passed as the Boulder Canyon Project Act in December 1928. More than two decades after President Roosevelt had described his vision of a "scheme of development" on the Colorado, a site had been found for a dam and the money authorized to build it. Then suddenly, the story of Hoover Dam began to unfold more quickly.

Over two days at the end of October 1929, the Dow Jones Industrial Average—a measure of the value of thirty industrial companies' stocks traded on the New York Stock Exchange—fell by 23 percent, and it continued to fall for the next two weeks, until it had lost nearly half its value.

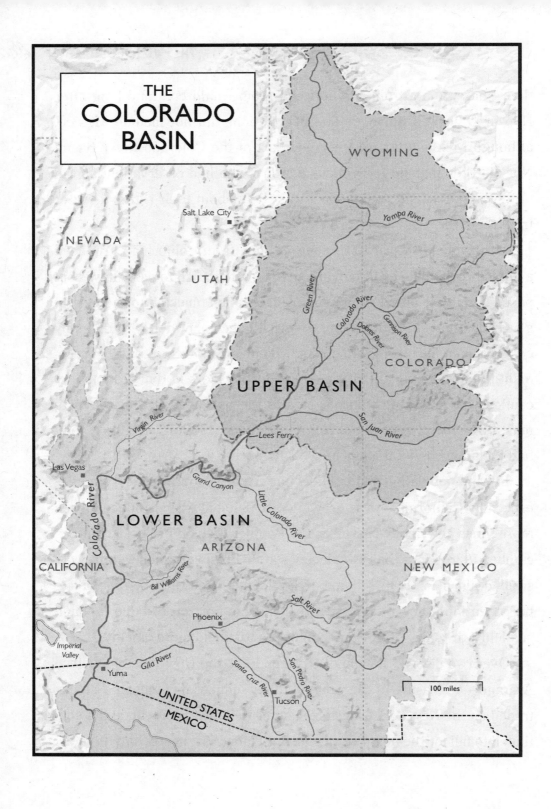

THE
COLORADO BASIN

WYOMING

Salt Lake City

NEVADA

UTAH

Yampa River

Green River

Colorado River

Dobres River

Gunnison River

COLORADO

UPPER BASIN

Virgin River

Lees Ferry

San Juan River

Las Vegas

Grand Canyon

Colorado River

Little Colorado River

LOWER BASIN

ARIZONA

NEW MEXICO

CALIFORNIA

Bill Williams River

Salt River

Phoenix

Imperial
Valley

Gila River

Yuma

Santa Cruz River

San Pedro River

Tucson

100 miles

UNITED STATES
MEXICO

The crash bankrupted investors and sent a shock through the country. It was the most dramatic sign that something was changing in America, that a period of prosperity was coming to an end. More than twenty-six thousand businesses closed in the year following the crash, putting their employees out of work, and 1,352 banks failed, causing their customers to lose their savings. The number of unemployed rose, reaching four million, or about 9 percent of the workforce, by the end of 1930.

At that moment, no one imagined what was to come: that the depression that began at the end of the 1920s would become the Great Depression of the 1930s, and almost a quarter of the American workforce would soon be unemployed. But the government saw that something needed to be done. "We should use the powers of government to cushion the situation," wrote President Herbert Hoover. In the weeks after the crash, he pressured business leaders, mayors, and governors to create jobs by increasing spending on construction, and in 1930 he asked Congress for an emergency fund of $150 million to speed up public works.

The biggest public works project of all was Hoover Dam, and the money for it had already been authorized by Congress. Here was something the government could do, and it ordered the Bureau of Reclamation to speed up the schedule so construction could be started and people put to

(Opposite) The Colorado River Basin covers almost 250,000 square miles. All the streams and rivers in the basin (shaded) eventually flow into the Colorado River and from there to the Gulf of California. In 1922, representatives of the seven US states with territory in the basin divided it into two parts, the upper and lower, at Lees Ferry, just north of the Grand Canyon. The upper basin consists of parts of · Wyoming, Colorado, Utah, New Mexico, and a small slice of Arizona. The lower basin contains parts of Nevada and California, most of Arizona, and small parts of Utah and New Mexico.

work. "In those days...people were standing on the street selling apples," said Walker Young. "People had been out of employment in all the United States, trying to recover from the deepest depression I believe we ever had. So every effort was made to get this project started as soon as possible."

At the Bureau of Reclamation, engineers hurried to produce blueprints and specifications. The government would build a railroad and a road to the construction site, and supply electricity, cement, steel, and other materials. But it wouldn't build the dam itself. For that, it would employ a private contractor, which would be responsible for hiring workers and providing machinery, moving everything to where it was needed, excavating and preparing the site, and building the dam, the power plant, and other structures. At the beginning of 1931, six months ahead of schedule, the Bureau of Reclamation published the plans and invited private contractors to submit bids for the job.

Meanwhile, on September 17, 1930, the United States secretary of the interior, Ray Lyman Wilbur, officially launched the Hoover Dam project by driving a silver railroad spike into the ground at Bracken, a few miles south of Las Vegas, at a ceremony to mark the start of construction of the railroad that would run to Black Canyon. Even though engineers were still working on plans for the dam, and thirty miles of empty desert lay between Wilbur and the place where it would be built, Wilbur declared Hoover Dam to be "one of man's greatest victories over nature."

(Top) September 17, 1930: The secretary of the interior, Ray Lyman Wilbur, drives a silver railroad spike, officially launching the Boulder Canyon Project. He missed on his first attempt, "missed it completely," said a local reporter. "He was not a spike driver; he was an administrator in a college."

(Bottom) January 1931: Crews lay track for a railroad from Las Vegas across the desert toward the dam construction site in Black Canyon.

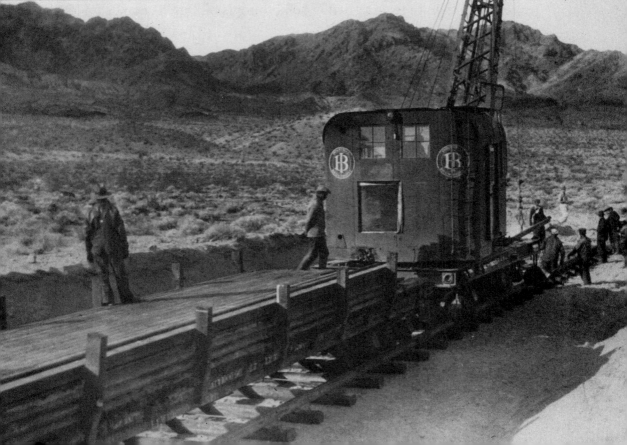

"The eyes of the entire construction world"

The plans for Hoover Dam specified a concrete arch-gravity dam. Gravity dams use their great weight to hold back water; the pressure of the water on the dam is transferred down to the bedrock through the dam's massive foundation. Arch dams use their shape to transfer the pressure sideways, against the walls of the canyon. Arch-gravity dams combine the strengths of both types. They are stronger and more reliable than arch dams, and lighter and cheaper to build than gravity dams. And concrete, which is stronger in compression (when something is pushing against it) than in tension (when something is pulling it) makes an ideal dam-building material.

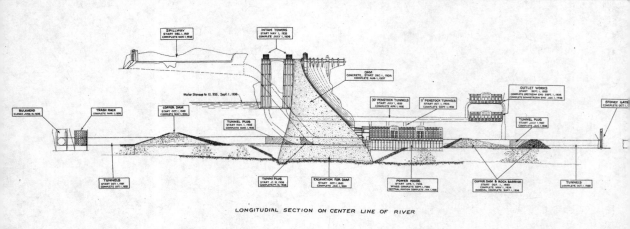

LONGITUDINAL SECTION ON CENTER LINE OF RIVER

Plans published in 1931 show Hoover Dam from the side and from above (opposite). The side view labels the dam's main features and shows the date by which the government expected them to be completed.

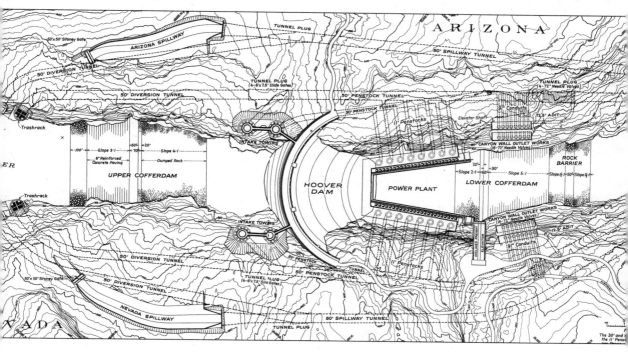

Seen from the side, Hoover Dam was wedge-shaped: 660 feet thick at the base, 45 feet at the top. From above, it was curved, with the apex of the curve facing upstream. It rose more than seven hundred feet from the bottom of the foundation to the roadway across the top. Downstream, at the foot of the dam, a powerhouse held sixteen electricity generators. Upstream, four intake towers would feed water through the dam, and two spillways would divert water around it in an emergency.

Before the plans were finalized, engineers at the Bureau of Reclamation designed, tested, and built models of dams in dozens of combinations of size and shape. But disaster also played a part in shaping them. On March 12, 1928, at three minutes before midnight, the St. Francis Dam forty miles north of Los Angeles collapsed. It disintegrated in seconds, sending a 140-foot-high wall of water racing without warning toward towns in the Santa Clarita Valley. By dawn, when the flood wave reached the Pacific Ocean, it had left behind a fifty-five-mile-long trail of destruction. More than 430 people died.

Investigators quickly discovered that St. Francis Dam had been poorly constructed on unsuitable rock, which had allowed water to seep around and underneath it, weakening its foundation. But it was the same type as Hoover Dam: a concrete arch-gravity dam. To reassure the public—and members of Congress, whose votes were needed to finance the project— the government appointed a board of engineers and geologists to review the plans. Hoover would be three-and-a-half times as tall as St. Francis and hold back about seven hundred times more water. "If it should fail," wrote the board, "the flood created would probably destroy Needles, Topock, Parker, Blythe, Yuma, and permanently destroy the levees of the Imperial district, creating a channel into Salton Sea which would proba- bly be so deep that it would be impracticable to reestablish the Colorado River in its normal course."

To avoid this terrible possibility, the board made several changes to Hoover Dam's design. To strengthen the dam, it changed the engi- neering specifications. To improve its ability to contain and control the Colorado River's annual floods, it increased the dam's height by twenty- five feet, and the capacity of its reservoir by 4.5 million acre-feet. And to handle emergencies, it enlarged the two spillways: Each would be able to divert two hundred thousand cubic feet of water per second—twice the equivalent of Niagara Falls—around the dam. The final design stood 726 feet tall, weighed more than 6.6 million tons, and was engineered to withstand a once-in-four-thousand-year flood. The reservoir would hold 30.5 million acre-feet of water—eighty thousand gallons for every man, woman, and child in the United States.

On the morning of March 4, 1931, a crowd of engineers, builders, newspaper reporters, and curious members of the public gathered in Denver to find out who would build this vast structure. It was the most expensive construction contract ever awarded by the US government, and the event was front-page news: "The eyes of the entire construction world as well as that of the whole southwestern part of the United States are focused on the Denver office of the bureau of reclamation," declared the *Las Vegas Evening Review and Journal*.

The government had received more than a hundred requests from contractors and others for plans for the project. Now, five had submitted bids to build it, each delivered in a sealed envelope. The lowest bid would win the contract.

With just five bids presented, people might have wondered if the project was so ambitious that only a foolhardy contractor would attempt it. And perhaps they were right: When the bid envelope from Edwin Smith of Kentucky was opened, it contained a letter to President Hoover proposing to build the dam for $88,000 less than anyone else and asking if government detectives could track down the company's engineer, who had gone missing. "But if you can't, we can get along without him," Smith wrote. More important, the envelope did not contain a check for the $2 million bid bond required by the government as a guarantee that the winning contractor would honor its bid. A second envelope also failed to include the bid bond. Both were disqualified.

That left three bids that met the government's requirements. The last to be opened was from Six Companies Inc., based in San Francisco, with a bid of $48,890,995.50. Six Companies' bid was $5 million less than the next lowest—and, it turned out, only $24,000 more than the government's own secret estimate of what the dam would cost. It won the contract to build Hoover Dam.

Six Companies was a group of companies that had formed a corporation together to bid for the job. They came from cities across the West: Salt Lake City, Boise, Portland, Oakland, Los Angeles, and San Francisco. Between them they had built every kind of big construction project: hundreds of miles of railroads crossing the forbidding deserts and mountain ranges between the Rockies and the Pacific, dams in remote mountain valleys, roads, bridges, water tunnels, concrete buildings reinforced to withstand earthquakes. But none of these projects was as big as Hoover Dam, and none of the companies was big enough to tackle it alone. Together they had the skills and experience—and, more important, the money. The government required a performance bond of $5 million as insurance that they would do the work.

Successfully building the dam would make the investors in Six Companies rich and transform their businesses into construction industry giants—but on that morning in March, that lay far in the future. As the crowd dispersed, contractors boarding trains home and newspaper reporters returning to their offices, the clock was already running. A week later, on March 11, the government officially awarded the contract for the construction of Hoover Dam to Six Companies. It required the contractor to finish the job in 2,565 days (seven years) and meet a series of deadlines along the way, with penalties to be paid for any that were missed.

For the dam builders, there wasn't a moment to lose.

CODA: NATIVE RIVER

When the Southern Pacific Railroad tried to stop the Colorado River flood in 1906, many of the white workers it hired soon quit because of the heat and the hard labor. Faced with rising floodwaters and a shortage of workers, the company pressed Indigenous men into work: About four hundred of them and their families camped near the river in the

Indigenous men working at the Colorado River break in 1906.

summer of 1906 and went to work on construction and boat crews. They were paid about a third less than whites, and they were likely forced to work. They belonged to several of the Indigenous peoples who had lived in the Colorado River Basin before the arrival of Europeans: the Quechan, who lived in the area where the river had burst its banks; the Cocopah, who lived to the south; the Kumeyaay from west of the river; and the Maricopa, Tohono O'odham, and Akimel O'odham from the east.

The white European Americans who came to the southwestern desert at the end of the 1800s were not the first to see that it could be irrigated and made to grow. A thousand years earlier, the Hohokam people built networks of irrigation canals along the Salt River and Gila River, which feed the Colorado from the east. The longest of their canals extended for around twenty miles, were precisely sloped—or graded—to maintain a steady flow of water without becoming clogged with silt, and watered thousands of acres of farmland. It is estimated that in 1300 CE as many as eighty thousand Hohokam were living in the area around what is now the city of Phoenix. One hundred and fifty years later their civilization had mostly disappeared, possibly because a change in the climate brought cycles of droughts and floods that destroyed the irrigation system.

The Indigenous peoples who lived to the west along the Colorado River itself did not build extensive irrigation systems: The unpredictable river would have destroyed them. Instead, they made use of the river's natural cycle of floods to water and fertilize their farmland. The Quechan lived next to the river for most of the year and moved to higher ground when the floods began in the late spring; when the water went down in the summer, they returned and planted crops. As well as soaking the earth, the flooding left behind silt that created a new layer of fertile soil every year, so the Quechan never needed to fertilize the land.

The river featured prominently in Quechan stories. They told how the world was once flooded by a being called Kwikumat and how both the people and the river were created when Kwikumat's son drove a spear into the earth. The Mojave, who lived farther north along the Colorado south of Black Canyon, told a similar creation story about Mastamho, who created the river by driving a stick into the ground. He floated down it in a boat, tilting it from side to side to make flat places in the valley for farming. The Mojave call themselves Pipa Aha Macav, the "people by the river."

Farming and trade, along with hunting and harvesting wild foods, supported life in the harsh world of the desert for the Quechan and Mojave and the other people who lived around the river in the 1600s and 1700s. The few Europeans who encountered them wrote of well-stocked villages and farms and a network of trade that supplied them with goods from the Pacific coast peoples to the west and the pueblo peoples to the east in what is now called New Mexico. But beginning in the mid-1800s, the Indigenous world of the Colorado River Valley was overrun by white European Americans from the east. White farmers seized land and brought cattle and other livestock, pushing out Indigenous crop farmers. Miners searching for silver and gold ignored how land had been used and left it scarred and spoiled. White roads, and then the railroads, brought more settlers; conflict between Indigenous people and the settlers brought the United States' military. The army built Fort Yuma on the Colorado River near the US-Mexican border in 1849 and Fort Mojave, two hundred miles upstream, in 1859.

Indigenous people were divided in how to respond: Some argued for cooperation, some for resistance and fighting the newcomers. But those who fought were not strong enough to force back the flood of white settlement. The last major conflict between them and the US Army took place in 1859. Afterward, Indigenous peoples were forced onto reservations: The Colorado River Reservation, shared between the Mojave and a branch of the Southern Paiute people, was established in 1865; the Fort Mojave Reservation, belonging to the Mojave, in 1870; the Fort Yuma Reservation, belonging to the Quechan, in 1884. At the same time, Indigenous children were made to attend cruelly administered "Indian schools," where they were given white names and taught English and forced to adopt the dress and customs of white people. When the US Army no longer needed Fort Yuma and Fort Mojave to subjugate Indigenous people by force, both were converted to Indian schools.

The US government also tried using irrigation to force Indigenous people to adopt white customs. The first federally financed irrigation project in United States history was a nine-mile-long canal dug to bring water to the Mojave reservation, finished in 1874. The government wanted to assimilate the Mojave by getting them to take up white-style homestead farming, but officials ignored Mojave leaders who told them the soil wasn't suitable, and the project failed.

Elsewhere, reservations were located in the same places that Indigenous people had lived before the arrival of whites, and for a time they continued using the river's yearly floods to water and refresh their land. But whites' efforts to divert the river for their own use interfered with traditional Indigenous ways of farming. One of the first projects to be built by the new Reclamation Service at the beginning of the 1900s was the Laguna Dam, finished in 1909. Water was diverted from the Colorado upstream from the Quechan lands in the Fort Yuma Reservation, reducing the river's flow, and new levees stopped the river from flooding Quechan lands naturally. The Quechan were promised water from the irrigation project, but the agency was slow to deliver it. Meanwhile, the US government sold parcels of what it considered surplus land on the reservation to non-Indigenous farmers.

As happened elsewhere in North America, the violence, loss of land, and disease brought by whites devastated the Quechan and other Indigenous people of the Colorado River Basin. By the beginning of the 1900s, the Quechan population had fallen to fewer than a thousand, from around four thousand in the mid-1800s. The Mojave and other peoples suffered similar declines. Without farming, hunting, and other traditional ways of life, they took wage-paying jobs on the railroad, in construction, in industry in new American towns such as Yuma—and, in the summer of 1906, on the Southern Pacific crews trying to stop the flooding of the Imperial Valley.

Although whites had taken Indigenous land, they hadn't taken the water. In 1908, the United States Supreme Court ruled that Indigenous reservation land included rights to water because the reservations were intended to provide a permanent homeland and water was necessary to support life. At the time, the court's ruling had little impact: It did not say how much water, and Indigenous peoples did not have the resources to put it to use. But as the twentieth century continued, demand for the

THE LOST CITY

In March 1932, as construction of Hoover Dam got underway, the *Los Angeles Times* urged its readers to visit what it called "one of the most remarkable ruins in the world."

"And if you ever expect to see it, you had better hurry," the paper said. "In all probability it will be submerged by the waters of the Hoover dam."

Pueblo Grande de Nevada was a network of pit and pueblo-style buildings located in the Moapa Valley seventy miles northeast of Las Vegas, built and occupied by Ancestral Puebloan people between about 300 and 1150 CE. The largest of the buildings had a hundred rooms. In the 1920s and '30s, they were studied by archaeologist Mark Harrington and an Indigenous colleague, Willis Evans. Harrington gave the ruins

(Opposite) A reconstructed building from the Lost City, Pueblo Grande de Nevada, with the rising waters of Lake Mead in the background, June 1938.

water increased and those rights became valuable. Water would turn out to mean not just life but new political and economic power for the Indigenous people of the Colorado River Basin.

the sensational name Lost City to attract funding and publicity and raced to catalog as much of them as possible before they were flooded. It was one of the few attempts made to preserve Indigenous sites as the waters rose. Reconstructions and some of the artifacts from the site can be seen today at the Lost City Museum in Overton, Nevada.

Men living in Ragtown, a rough settlement next to the Hoover Dam construction site, in 1931. As the Great Depression took hold, unemployed men and their families flooded into Nevada, and the US government accelerated the schedule for building the dam to create jobs. But thousands more people were looking for work than there were jobs available. There was no housing, and the summer heat was almost unendurable. To stay ahead of deadlines, Six Companies pushed the work forward, sometimes with little regard for safety.

TWO

BOSSES AND MEN

"He had a memory like an elephant"

MARCH 11, 1931. THE SAME DAY THAT THE US GOVERNMENT OFFICIALLY awarded the contract to build Hoover Dam to Six Companies, a tall man wearing a pressed white shirt and a Stetson hat stepped off a train in Las Vegas. His name was Frank Crowe, and his arrival was closely watched. The Depression that had begun more than a year earlier was steadily worsening, and for months unemployed men had been gathering in the town. Crowe was the man who was going to put them to work. "Dam Job Head Here Wednesday," read a headline running the width of the front page of the *Las Vegas Evening Review and Journal* on March 9. The paper reported that as many as three thousand jobs would soon be available. "Crowe and his gang of muckers and granite blasters won't be able to get into the Nevada waste lands quick enough," the report cheered.

Crowe was the construction superintendent for Six Companies. He had a reputation for building dams fast and making his employers money, and a nickname to go with it: Hurry-Up Crowe.

Superintendent Frank Crowe at the site of Boulder City on March 13, 1931, two days after he arrived to begin work on Hoover Dam.

"Any time you saw a white shirt and a large Stetson hat coming, you knew that was Frank Crowe," said Bob Parker, who was seventeen years old when he started working at the damsite a few weeks after Crowe arrived. "Very tall and erect, kind of a stately looking person, a very likable fellow." But like everyone who worked for Six Companies, Bob learned not to get on the wrong side of the superintendent. "He never forgot you if you ever crossed him. Men that had worked for him fifteen, twenty years before this dam started, if they ever did anything wrong, he knew it. He remembered it; he never forgot. He had a memory like an elephant."

Marion Allen, the driller's nipper, said that Crowe was the sort of boss who would give a man a job and a chance, but it was up to him to keep it. "That's the type he was. He'd give you a boost, but you'd better look out for yourself." Crowe's power was absolute: Fail to show up, loaf around, or talk back, and you'd be out of a job, "walking down the road talking to yourself," said Marion.

Crowe was the country's most experienced dam builder. He joined the Reclamation Service after graduating from college in 1905 and had worked on more than a dozen different dam projects. On five of them, he was the chief engineer. Building a dam in Wyoming in 1911, he saved money and time by having his crews work around the clock in three shifts, instead of one, and he organized the project so different parts were completed simultaneously, instead of one after the other. At another dam, built in Idaho the next year, Crowe turned to engineering to save time: He replaced slow wagons with a system of aerial cableways that could deliver concrete to any point on the construction site in a few seconds. The system was so efficient that for a while the builders couldn't make concrete fast enough to keep up with it. But in the mid-1920s the Bureau of Reclamation stopped building dams itself and started hiring private contractors to do the work. Crowe went to work for one of them, called Morrison-Knudsen, which would become part of Six Companies.

Crowe was the reason Six Companies won the contract to build Hoover Dam. "Each of the six firms knew that they had to get a genius to do the job," remembered the editor of the *Boulder City Journal*, Elton Garrett. "They knew the thing to do was get together on an agreement, get Frank Crowe on the job, have him ramrod it. And that's what they did."

Not only was Crowe experienced, but he was shrewd. The other bidders for the contract estimated the cost of materials and labor, then added money for profit and to cover mistakes and the unexpected. Crowe's estimate of the costs was lower to begin with, and he also assumed he'd find ways to save money as the work went on. "You can bid at your figured cost on the theory you're sufficiently smart to cut enough corners to make a substantial profit," he said later. But that meant working fast and getting the most out of machines and men. "He not only wanted good work but a lot of it per shift," said Walker Young.

Crowe didn't waste a minute. The day he arrived in Las Vegas he drove to Black Canyon and took a boat down the river to look at the damsite. It wasn't the first time he'd been there, but now Bureau of Reclamation surveyors had painted white lines on the walls of the canyon showing where the dam he was going to build would rise.

With him was Walker Young. If Crowe's job was to build the dam and make a profit for Six Companies, Young's job was to make sure it was done right. He was now the Bureau of Reclamation's chief construction engineer for Hoover Dam. He and his team of engineers and inspectors would make sure plans and specifications were followed and approve every stage of construction—and if a change was needed, they would have to approve that, too.

In the early years of the twentieth century, building dams was one of the busiest and most exciting careers available to an engineer, and like Crowe, Young had joined the Reclamation Service out of college to be part of it. He was careful and precise and paid attention to every aspect of the job.

The government's chief construction engineer, Walker Young, in his office in Boulder City in 1932.

"Walker Young was a man that was a stickler for detail," remembered Bob Parker. "Sometimes he'd speak and talk a leg off of you. The next time he came down to sit in the chair, he might not say three words all the time he was down there. But he was watching everything that was going on."

"They came with everything on their backs"

As Frank Crowe made his way to Las Vegas in the spring of 1931, so did thousands of others.

Erma and Tom Godbey came from Arizona. Tom was a miner, and with so many men out of work, mineowners were reducing pay "just because they could," according to Erma. "They were still paying fourteen percent dividend to their stockholders, but they were cutting men's wages." In June, the Godbeys loaded their four children and what possessions they could fit into a car and set out for the damsite. "It was just dirt roads and it was plenty hot," Erma said.

High scaler Joe Kine lost his job when the mine he worked at in Oklahoma closed. He picked strawberries and tried work as a salesman selling pantyhose. Hearing that there was work at the dam, he bought a used Model T Ford for $10 and drove from Missouri to southern Nevada, where he sold the car for $2.50 so he could eat. Thirteen-year-old Harold Wadman ran away from home in Utah with ten cents and two jars of cherries that he stole from his mom's pantry. He was afraid to try jumping a freight train, so he hitchhiked to Las Vegas. Curley Francis had been working on a construction crew in California, camping out and hunting rabbits. "That was the only way we kept eating most of the time," he said. When he heard that the contractor he'd been working for was part of Six Companies, he headed east looking for work.

Some of the new arrivals stayed in Las Vegas, where hundreds camped in parks in front of the railroad station and the courthouse. Others made their way to Black Canyon, to makeshift camps near the construction site. When the government planned the dam, one of its requirements was that the construction company that built it would provide housing for its workers and that the housing would be ready when construction started. But then the Depression began, the government sped up the schedule to create jobs, and this requirement was set aside. When Six Companies started hiring workers in April 1931, it hadn't built housing for them. The government had also assumed that most of the workers would be single men, but the beginning of the Depression changed that, too. As people lost their jobs, homes, and savings, entire families moved in search of work. Many went to Nevada, to the camps in the desert near Hoover Dam.

Murl Emery, who operated a boat service on the Colorado River, watched them arrive. "They'd come with their kids," he said. "They came

A woman outside her tent home near the site of Hoover Dam, March 13, 1931.

with everything on their backs. And their cars had broke down before they got here, and they walked." Rough settlements sprang up along the road between Las Vegas and Black Canyon and around the government surveying and construction camps. The biggest was on the banks of the Colorado at the northern end of Black Canyon, in an area called Hemenway Wash. It became known as Ragtown because of the tents, or sometimes Hell's Hole because of the heat. Around fourteen hundred people lived there in the summer of 1931, in whatever shelter they had: tents, shacks made of wooden crates and flattened oilcans, or their cars. If they had nothing, they hung a sack or a blanket over a rope or the branches of a mesquite bush to make a little shade.

Ragtown looked like what it was: a place thrown together from trash and canvas in the middle of a baked, dusty desert, miles from anywhere. When Velma Holland arrived there at night with her family after driving from Detroit, she was fooled by the moon shining on the river. "It was the most beautiful silver strand you ever saw in your life," she recalled. But in daylight things were different: "We got up the next morning. I looked out, and right down there it was awful—tents, big wood-colored stuff that had looked so beautiful the night before in the moonlight."

There was no running water and no sanitation. People scooped water from the river, then waited for the silt to settle in the bottom of the bucket so they could use it. They bathed and washed their clothes in the river, but they had to be careful: The current could catch people, especially small children, and sweep them away; the silt would collect in clothes and shoes and weigh them down, making it hard to swim. Toilets

Ragtown, summer 1931, with the bank of the Colorado River on the left.

were holes dug in the ground. Sometimes there were lines to use them because dirty water and food that spoiled in the heat made people sick.

The first grocery store in the area opened in April in a tent beside the road from Las Vegas. People bought their food there or from Murl Emery's general store at the boat landing. The alternative was a sixty-mile round trip to Las Vegas. Murl charged people what they told him they would have paid for the same groceries back home, in whatever part of the country

A family in front of their home in Ragtown, August 1931.

Children in Ragtown.

they came from, and when he wasn't there, they took what they needed and left money on the counter. Most food was canned. There was no refrigeration, so fresh food went bad, and anything left out immediately attracted pests. People positioned table legs in cans of water to stop the ants from climbing them and getting to the food before they could.

The first grocery store in the area offered "Home Farm Products," which were mostly canned goods.

They cooked on fires or camping stoves and burned their garbage. In the dry country, open flames were a constant danger to the tents and wooden shacks. In March, a fire tore through part of Ragtown. "The flames during the blaze were at times 50 feet high, fanned by a high wind which rushed down the canyon," reported the *Las Vegas Evening Review and Journal*. No one was hurt, but six families were left homeless, and lost the few possessions they had.

Families in Ragtown were also living on a construction site. One night, Murl Emery had an uneasy feeling about the blasting for the railroad track being laid into Black Canyon. He woke people and moved them away from the area. Minutes later, an explosion showered their homes with rocks. The worker who had set the charge raced to the camp, thinking he'd killed everybody, "and he damn near would have," said Murl, "but I'd helped them out."

Cars and furniture destroyed by a fire that burned through part of Ragtown in March 1931.

But it wasn't construction, fire, or bad water that mostly killed people. It was the heat. The average temperature in Black Canyon for the month of July 1931 was 107.4 degrees, and on two out of every three days that month the high temperature was over 120 degrees. "It just seemed like it was so terrible hot," said Helen Holmes, who had come from Wyoming. "Sometimes you'd feel like you couldn't get your breath." Parents wrapped their children in wet sheets so they could sleep, and let them go without clothes to keep cool during the day—but they got sunburned, and the blisters from the sunburns got infected. On a single day that summer, July 26, four people died in Ragtown. One of them, a neighbor of Erma Godbey, tied a note to her dog's collar and sent the dog to look for help, but by the time the dog returned with a ranger she was dead. For Erma, it was the last straw. "I told my husband, 'We've got to get out of here. We've just absolutely got to get out of here. I've got to get somewhere I can get the babies to a doctor if need be, and also myself.'" She and Tom moved to a campground in Las Vegas, and Tom commuted to his job on a road construction crew.

Others waited. Eight miles to the west of the damsite, on a stretch of high desert where the air was a little cooler, surveyors were laying out the streets of a new town, Boulder City, and Six Companies had begun building accommodations there for its employees. The first permanent housing was finished at the end of July: two dormitories for single men, and thirty cottages for families. Slowly, people began moving out of Ragtown and the other temporary camps, although it would be several months before there was enough housing for them all.

Meanwhile, there were the tents and the heat, the pests and the canned food, the dust blowing in the desert wind, and the muddy river to bathe in. "You were really just existing," said Helen Holmes.

"Don't go down there"

Getting out of Ragtown meant getting a job, but there were many more people in the camps and in Las Vegas than there were jobs available. Six Companies began hiring workers at the beginning of April 1931—but not the thousands that were hoped for. That month, there were just a few hundred people on Six Companies' payroll. A month later, in May, there were about a thousand, and by August, thirteen hundred. It wasn't until the end of the year that the number employed by Six Companies passed three thousand. The company received forty-two thousand applications for those jobs—more than a dozen for every one person employed.

The government told people not to travel to the area to look for work: "None should go to Las Vegas unless he is assured of employment upon arrival, or is equipped with independent means to carry him over a period of several months," it advised. As far away as New York, newspapers repeated the warning that there was "already a serious problem in caring for those here seeking work."

The *Las Vegas Age* called conditions in the town "pitiful" and reported that families were close to starving. A girl of three told reporters she had eaten "a great big spoonful of mush" that morning. "It tasted good because they didn't have anything yesterday," she said. The girl's mother said she couldn't send her children to school because they had no food other than an occasional loaf of bread and no shoes. The paper pleaded for the Red Cross to come help and for the government to give priority to hiring married men on the dam job so that they could support their families.

Helen Holmes and her husband, Neil, heard the warnings as they traveled from Wyoming. "When we was on the way down here, people would ask us where we were going," said Neil. "We told them Boulder City and Las Vegas to work on the dam. They said, 'Don't go down there. You haven't got a chance to get on. There's thousands of people wrestling jobs down there.'"

Neil had worked for Frank Crowe before and had a letter guaranteeing him a job: He started work the day after he and Helen arrived. Those who hadn't arranged a job in advance joined the crowd outside the employment office, across the street from the courthouse in Las Vegas. "Everybody would line up in the front of that window in the morning and go to it, and they said, 'Well, we need ten muckers and we need fifteen drillers,'" remembered Jake Dieleman. Some applied more than once, using different names, with the idea that more names on the list meant more chances of getting a job. But they had to keep track of the names they'd used, and not forget and miss out if one of them was called.

Others skipped the line at the employment office and went directly to the jobsite, where they'd find someone in charge and try to talk their way into getting hired. "You just went out on the job and hustled the

Looking for work: The crowd outside the employment office in Las Vegas, spring 1931.

foreman," explained John Gieck, from California. John followed one of Six Companies' foremen around for "five or six days" before the man relented and gave him a job.

The reason that Six Companies didn't hire more men in the spring of 1931 was that it could not put them to work. The government was building a road and a railroad from Las Vegas to the damsite, and stringing a two-hundred-mile-long power transmission line from California to provide electricity. Until the road and the railroad were finished, workers and materials couldn't reach the construction site easily, and until the power line was finished, they had only portable gas-powered compressors to run their jackhammers and other tools, and no lights for the night shift.

Only the electricity arrived without difficulty. The transmission line was finished and the power switched on at the end of June. (Later, when Hoover Dam was finished and the power plant there began making electricity, the current was reversed, and the same line carried power back to California.)

The railroad reached the site of Boulder City, twenty-three miles from Las Vegas, in February, five months after it was started. But the last section, covering the remaining seven miles between Boulder City and Black Canyon, took another seven months to build. The line wound through closely packed mountain ridges and gullies so rough that in some places the only way to get dynamite and tools to where they were needed was on the backs of burros. Crews had to build viaducts across the gullies, blast cuts through the ridges, and dig five tunnels to get the line to its destination on the canyon rim.

Where it ended, the government railroad was still high above the river. To reach the bottom of the canyon, Six Companies began building its own railroad, joining the government line between Boulder City and the construction site, looping through Hemenway Wash and past Ragtown, and into Black Canyon from the north. Starting in April, Six Companies crews blasted and excavated their way slowly along the river toward the damsite, grading a railroad bed and laying down track along the canyon walls. As the canyon narrowed and the walls got steeper, they dug tunnels through rock outcrops and the line clung precariously to the cliffs.

Like the government railroad, the government highway traveled smoothly across the desert from Las Vegas to Boulder City, then had to

April 1931: One of the first photos taken of the construction of Hoover Dam shows a shovel excavating the railroad bed into Black Canyon.

fight its way through the mountains to Black Canyon. There, it stopped suddenly on the edge of the canyon, waiting for the dam to be finished so it could continue over the top to Arizona. The road was finished in July, but it required train car loads of dynamite to force its way through the hard, volcanic rock, and sometimes the work moved forward only inches in a day. "I couldn't believe rock could get that hard," said the contractor who built the road.

Meanwhile, Six Companies pushed work forward as fast as it could. Small crews were ferried into the canyon by boat to begin excavating

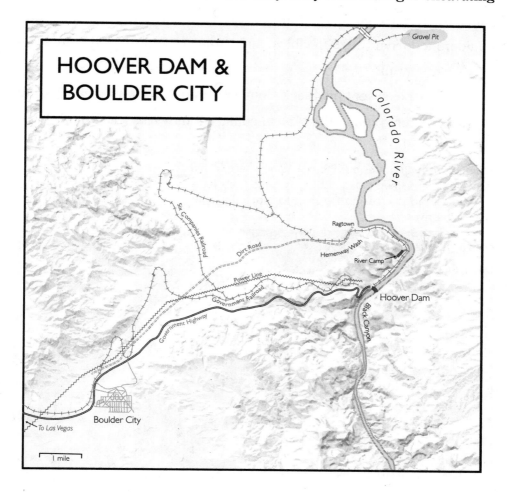

access tunnels in the walls called adits and to prepare foundations for the compressor plants that would power machinery and the mixing plants that would make concrete. They landed equipment on a small beach on the Arizona side of the river and cut a shelf out of the rock opposite on the Nevada side and built a footbridge to connect them. To reach the most remote worksites high on the canyon walls, they built strings of ladders, and some camped out on the job because of the difficulty getting there and back every day. Six Companies hurriedly built dormitories for four hundred men, a kitchen, and a dining hall right on the side of the canyon. The buildings, called River Camp, perched uneasily on stilts. Sometimes boulders fell from the cliffs above and came crashing into the dormitories' wooden walls.

As the weeks went by, Black Canyon began to fill with men. *Fortune* magazine later compared a typical construction worker at Hoover Dam

When construction began, there was nowhere for work crews or equipment to land along the steep sides of Black Canyon. By June 1931, there were ladders and a footbridge crossing the river to reach the opening of an adit in the wall above the river.

River Camp, June 1931.

to a soldier: "His average age is thirty-three. His average wage is sixty-eight cents an hour. He is taller and heavier than the average U.S. soldier, runs a greater risk of losing his life, and has passed a more drastic physical examination." But as the work got going in the spring of 1931, many of those men were also hungry, homeless, and desperate. Some were used to construction work, but some were inexperienced, doing hard physical labor for the first time: "People well-off in their normal lives," recalled a reporter, "half-destitute or almost all destitute because of the

Depression, coming in and looking for a job, happy to get an ordinary common laborer's job."

In the harsh working conditions and unbearable heat of Black Canyon, desperation, hunger, and hurry were a dangerous combination.

"That siren—oh, it scared you"

"Eleven Escape Death in Terrific Dynamite Explosion in River Canyon," reported the *Las Vegas Age* on May 9. One crew was at work on the lower level of the canyon wall when another working above them set off a blast without warning.

"Two men, P. L. Lezie and Herman Schmitto, received injuries from which it is thought will cause their death," said the paper. "Lezie received the full force of the terrific blast being blown some fifty feet and almost into the river....Schmitto was struck in the head and shoulder by rock and is believed to be suffering from a fractured skull. His ear was also almost severed from his head." The injured men were brought out of the canyon by boat, only to find that one of the ambulances sent for them had blown a tire, didn't have a spare, and couldn't complete the trip. Lezie made the journey to a hospital in Las Vegas in the bed of a pickup truck.

Schmitto and Lezie survived, but a little over a week later, on May 17, two men were killed when the section of canyon wall where they were working collapsed, crushing them "beyond recognition," according to the *Age*.

Accidents continued into the summer. On June 2: "Narrowly escaping what might have been a painful death, Alfred Peterson, 48, a powder man employed at the Boulder dam project, was buried under a landslide."

On June 20: "Two Men Killed, 3 Hurt in Dam Tunnel." One of the men was tapping a dynamite charge into a hole in preparation for a blast, and his blows were said to have been "too vigorous."

On July 18: "A. B. Oliver was severely burned about the hands and arms when some gasoline with which he was cleaning compressor bearings exploded. Authorities say this is the third instance they have observed of gasoline exploding in the open air."

In Ragtown, the men's families were close enough to hear the alarms that sounded when there was an accident and worried that their turn might be next. "That siren—oh, it scared you 'cause you wondered if it might be your husband," remembered Helen Holmes. The families of men killed or injured on the job received payments from workers' compensation funds administered by the states of Nevada and Arizona and paid for by Six Companies' insurance premiums. But an injury—or worse—meant losing a job and a steady income and having to leave and face an uncertain future.

Twenty-six men died on the construction site between the middle of May and the beginning of August. The biggest number—sixteen deaths—were from heatstroke. Inside the canyon, where the air was trapped by the high walls and there was little breeze, it was even hotter than in Ragtown. Men quickly became dehydrated, and their body temperatures could rise dangerously, leading to vomiting, convulsions, and unconsciousness.

"We dashed out there with these ice buckets, and we'd pack them in ice," said Bob Parker, who worked in the kitchen at River Camp. "If their heart took it and they survived, okay. But if their heart stopped, that was it. We sent for the undertaker."

There were "many, many of them taken out," said Neil Holmes. "Probably fifteen or twenty a day....They hauled them out just as fast as they'd come." Some who reached the hospital in Las Vegas had temperatures as high as 112 degrees. They were put in bathtubs filled with ice water until their temperatures dropped and were given injections of fluids to rehydrate their bodies. Often it was too late. On June 28, Mike Mada collapsed at the end of his shift. "There was a swelling of the brain and a resultant pressure. His breath was spasmodic," doctors reported. "It was impossible to do anything for him, his condition being such that he passed away immediately."

For men living in Ragtown or at River Camp, there was no escape and no chance for their bodies to recover when their shifts ended. Even at night, temperatures in July didn't drop much below 95 degrees. At River Camp there were no air coolers or fans, and no electricity. The drinking water was warm. It sometimes went bad and made men sick because it was drawn directly from the river and was stored outside in a concrete tank in the heat. Latrines filled the camp with a foul smell. There were no showers, and it could be dangerous to bathe in the river. In July, two men were swept away and drowned.

Six Companies began bringing fresh drinking water by tanker from Las Vegas and installed a watercooler—but it was small and couldn't keep up with the men's thirst. Instead of improving conditions at River

This photograph of a burning truck in Black Canyon was published in Six Companies' official history of Hoover Dam with the caption: "It doesn't take much to start fires at 128 degrees in the shade."

Camp, the company concentrated its efforts on the new dormitories and dining hall it was building in Boulder City, which were equipped with air-conditioning, fans, and showers. But it was hiring men faster than it could provide accommodation for them, and in Black Canyon the work went on in punishing conditions. During the workday, the heat made men slow and accident-prone. At mealtimes, men who had been hungry for months found they had lost their appetites. At night, they struggled to sleep.

"If I hadn't been a young fellow, I'd have never managed to make it," said Bob Parker.

"They will work under our conditions, or they will not work at all"

Despite the conditions, working at the dam was something more than a job in hard times. For many, being part of what was to become the biggest and most famous construction project in the United States was also a matter of pride. A journalist who visited the site that August later wrote, "Boulder Dam, with all its hardships and dangers, makes a challenge one can take pride in meeting....And the men felt this pride, too." But he added, "The trouble was that as time went on, they found that they were not really working for the United States, but for a group of construction companies."

On Friday, August 7, men arrived at work to find that wages for some of them were to be cut by as much as a dollar a day. Six Companies said that new machinery had made the men's work less valuable and that only thirty would be affected. The workers believed that closer to 180 men would have their pay cut and that the company was getting ready to reduce everyone's wages, knowing that there were so many unemployed men nearby who would work for less.

"They were going to cut the wages on the muckers in the tunnels," said Erma Godbey. "The other men that did the other kinds of work knew that if they were successful in cutting the muckers' wages, they would cut their wages, too."

That evening, Black Canyon fell quiet for the first time since April. The workers held meetings at River Camp and the new camp in Boulder

City and voted to walk off the job. The next morning representatives of the striking men met with Frank Crowe and presented him with their demands for going back to work. They included restoring pay to the original rates, improvements to the latrines and washrooms at River Camp, a supply of ice water, and requiring Six Companies to follow the mining safety laws of Nevada and Arizona, which the contractor had been able to avoid because the damsite was located on federal land. Crowe told them he would respond the following day.

Workers meeting in Boulder City in August 1931, where they voted to strike in protest over wage cuts and conditions at the jobsite.

Among the organizers of the strike were members of a labor union called the Industrial Workers of the World, better known by the nickname Wobblies. The long-term goal of the Wobblies was revolutionary change in American industry that would replace capitalist bosses and put workers in control. Their short-term goal was to organize workers on projects like Hoover Dam to advocate for safe conditions and fair pay. Neither made them welcome to Six Companies, which did not recognize and refused to negotiate with labor unions. Frank Crowe told the press that he believed the strike was "largely the result of I.W.W. agitation" and that "the company would be glad to be rid of such." In Las Vegas, Wobblies selling the union newspaper were arrested and jailed. Sheriff's deputies transported men they believed to be union organizers across the California state line and left them there, with men stationed "to see that they didn't come back."

Some of the striking men were suspicious of the union, too, afraid that the Wobblies' reputation as revolutionaries and troublemakers would be a distraction in their argument with Six Companies for better conditions. "We're not wobblies, and don't want to be classed as such," they told Crowe and the press. But others saw the union as helping to put pressure on Six Companies when individual workers couldn't. "They needed the troublemakers to make the contractor do what he should do for the men," said one.

On Sunday, August 9, Frank Crowe gave the strikers their answer: No.

Six Companies would not agree to any of their demands and planned to remove them from River Camp and Boulder City and hire replacement workers. In San Francisco, Crowe's boss, Six Companies president William Wattis, told the press, "They will work under our conditions or they will not work at all."

The strikers didn't trust Six Companies, but they believed the United States government would listen to them and wouldn't take sides in the dispute, and at first it seemed they were right. When Six Companies sent armed men to try and remove the strikers occupying River Camp and Boulder City, the government stepped in. The damsite and the camps were on federal property, and marshals disarmed the men and told them that they had no authority there. The strikers were allowed to remain. Meanwhile, strike leaders telegrammed the secretary of labor in Washington for support: "As American citizens, we ask protection on Hoover Dam in case of deportation. Strike called in protest against wage cuts."

The appeal went unheard. On Tuesday, a "pale-looking" Walker Young went to the camps and told the men they would have to leave. "If you should refuse to go, we'll—make you," he said. Because Young represented the government and not Six Companies, the men agreed. In a sudden rainstorm, they climbed into trucks and left to set up camp outside government land, on the highway near Las Vegas, where they could see and protest any attempt by Six Companies to bring in replacement workers.

On Thursday, Young ordered Six Companies to hire new workers and start work again. A new employment office was opened near Boulder City, and men quickly gathered there to apply for jobs. The strikers continued to protest, but with men going hungry and so many unemployed available to replace them, they had little power to fight without the government's support. On August 16 they voted to end the strike. "A man with a wife and children can't let his family starve," one of them told a journalist.

Most of those who had walked out got their jobs back—although not the union organizers: "There was no discrimination against the strikers," reported the *Las Vegas Evening Review-Journal*, "except those known to carry 'red' cards and bear a reputation as agitators." While Six Companies had publicly refused the strikers' demands, it quietly fixed some of the problems that had led to the strike. When men returned to River Camp, they found cooling equipment, lights, and new watercoolers being installed.

But the pay cut remained, and the failed strike had shown that Six Companies could set conditions at Hoover Dam and the government would support it.

And there was another, visible outcome of the strike: a newly built guardhouse and gate across the highway at the edge of the federal land that contained the construction site and Boulder City. From then on,

The gate and guardhouse on the highway to Boulder City and Hoover Dam.

anyone wishing to visit the site or the new town would need to show identification and state their business. Those not welcome included people the authorities considered a bad influence, such as liquor sellers and gamblers—and union men.

CODA: ALL-AMERICAN RIVER

There were two parts to the Hoover Dam project. The biggest and best-known was the concrete barrier being built in Black Canyon. But the act of Congress that authorized and funded its construction included a second piece: an eighty-mile-long canal three hundred miles to the south, in the Colorado Desert near Yuma, to deliver water from the Colorado River to the Imperial Valley.

Hoover Dam would control flooding, store water, and generate electricity. But it had another purpose: "to preserve American rights in the flow of the river," in the words of President Hoover. Ever since water had been diverted from the Colorado in 1901, it had been channeled south of the US-Mexican border through Mexico, in a dry riverbed that had been renamed the Imperial Canal, before turning north across the border into the Imperial Valley. In return for being allowed to operate in Mexico, the US owners of the irrigation system agreed that farmers in Mexico would be entitled to half of the water diverted along the canal.

This situation made people in California's Imperial Valley uneasy. All the valley's water had to pass through Mexico. They feared that farms south of the border would use increasing amounts of it, limiting the opportunity for growth in the north, or perhaps all of it, drying up the supply entirely. They complained that owners of land in Mexico didn't contribute to the maintenance of the irrigation system and that the amount they paid for the water didn't cover the cost of supplying it. Mexicans, in turn, distrusted the northerners, especially because much of the farmland south of the border was actually owned by US landowners who leased the land to non-Mexican farmers. In 1910, a revolution broke out in Mexico, which led to fighting that threatened operation of the irrigation canal; it raised fears in the United States of a less friendly Mexican government taking control of the water supply.

The answer, according to Imperial Valley farmers, was a new "all-American" canal, north of the border. At first, this was opposed by the Bureau of Reclamation, which wanted to develop a water management scheme for the entire Colorado River, not just the Imperial Valley. It was also opposed by other states—especially Arizona. They were afraid that California would use the canal to claim more than its share of the water from the river. But once planning for Hoover Dam began, the canal was made part of it, and when the Boulder Canyon Project Act was passed by Congress in 1928, it included funding to build the All-American Canal to divert water to the Imperial Valley before it crossed the border into Mexico.

Because the river originated in the United States, the government believed that the country was entitled to use as much of the water as it chose and that it had no obligation to leave any for Mexico. "I shall oppose any kind of agreement recognizing any kind of Mexican water right in the Colorado River until it is definitely and fully determined that there is a surplus of water in that stream for which there is no possible use in the United States," then-Representative Carl Hayden of Arizona said in 1922 during the first congressional hearings on funding the Boulder Canyon project.

Mexico saw things differently. The Colorado River ran through its territory to the ocean, and farmers in the Mexicali Valley depended on it to irrigate their crops. Freight could be carried on the river by boat as far north as the border. All of that was threatened by Hoover Dam and the All-American Canal, and after the Boulder Canyon Project Act was passed, Mexico sought a treaty with the United States that would ensure the river continued to cross the border. Mexico wanted a guarantee of 4.5 million acre-feet of water per year—enough for all the farmland in its territory that could be irrigated by the Colorado, about a quarter of the water estimated to flow down the river in a year. The United States offered a sixth of Mexico's figure, 750,000 acre-feet—enough to irrigate only the land already being farmed. Negotiations broke down. Mexico's distrust of the United States grew when US congressmen circulated a proposal to buy Mexico's territory in the Colorado River Basin in 1931.

Construction of the canal would begin in 1934 while Hoover Dam was rising in Black Canyon. Draglines—giant scoops attached to power cranes—began excavating a 160-foot-wide trench across the Colorado Desert. The Depression, combined with a drought in the 1930s, had left many people unemployed in the Imperial Valley. To provide jobs, men were put to work grading the canal with horse- and mule-drawn scrapers called Fresnos. When it was finished in 1940, the canal drew an almost straight line across the desert, before making a loop around the town of Calexico and connecting to the valley's irrigation network. It was cause

Draglines excavating the All-American Canal, 1936.

for a celebration. On October 12, a dedication ceremony near Calexico began with a person dressed as the Roman god of the sea, Neptune, arriving on a barge and ended with dancing in the streets. And even before the All-American Canal reached the Imperial Valley, work had begun on an extension: an additional 123 miles to carry Colorado River water north to the Coachella Valley, where farmers had depended on wells to irrigate their land.

The All-American Canal ran parallel to the international boundary, in many places just a stone's throw away. But the water was now north of the border, and with Hoover Dam to store it and the canal to divert and deliver it, the United States had control of the Colorado River.

A man and a power shovel in the entrance to one of the tunnels that diverted the Colorado River around the damsite during construction. Before the dam could be built, the river had to be moved out of the way and the riverbed and canyon walls excavated and scoured. Drilling the four diversion tunnels—each fifty feet in diameter and almost a mile long—and turning the river through them was the most difficult, dangerous, and expensive part of the entire project.

THREE

TURNING THE RIVER

*"He would fire a man for even looking like he
was going to slow down"*

DECEMBER 13, 1931. IT WAS MARION ALLEN'S FIRST DAY AT WORK. HE
had a slip of paper that stated his job—nipper—and what he would be
paid—$5 a day. Marion had been a carpenter, but when he arrived from
Wyoming looking for work at the dam, there were no jobs available for
carpenters, so he was assigned to a tunneling crew instead. Being underground made Marion nervous, and he had no idea what a nipper's job
was. The minute he got outside the Six Companies office he asked. Hauling steel and dynamite, he was told. "Then I really did wonder what I was
getting into!" Marion said.

Two hours after he was hired, Marion was aboard a truck for the
seven-mile trip from Boulder City to the construction site. There, a boat
took him down the river and set him ashore at the entrance to a huge
tunnel that disappeared into the canyon wall. Men were everywhere, and
dump trucks and other machinery roared back and forth. "I had never

seen so many working men going in so many different directions," Marion remembered. "It looked to me like most of them were lost."

Marion found his crew in a long wooden building called the change room. He found the foreman there, too—"a man so tough he could bite a nail in two and would fire a man for even looking like he was going to slow down," Marion said later. On a word from the foreman—"Let's go!"—the men took off, some of them running. Marion hurried along into the gaping mouth of the tunnel. "I was afraid if I slowed down I'd be trampled."

The first phase of construction of Hoover Dam was now fully underway. Before the dam itself could be built, the Colorado River had to be temporarily diverted. Marion was on his way to work in one of the four tunnels that would carry the water around the construction site through the walls of Black Canyon. Each was fifty feet in diameter and almost a mile long. Dynamite, bulldozers, power shovels, and men with jackhammers and picks were forcing their way through the rock. When these tunnels were complete, a temporary dam called a cofferdam would be built across the river, forcing it out of its natural channel and into the mouths of the tunnels. Only with the Colorado moved aside and its bed dry and exposed could men go to work building the main dam.

The US government's contract with Six Companies called for the diversion tunnels to be finished and the river diverted in less than two years, by October 1, 1933. If Six Companies missed the deadline, it faced a stiff penalty: $3,000 per day.

In reality, Six Companies didn't have that long. The only time of year it was possible to divert the Colorado was in the late fall and winter, when the water level was low and the river was quiet. In the spring and summer, when the river was swollen with water from melting snow, it was too powerful and too dangerous. So Six Companies had to finish the tunnels and turn the river several months ahead of the government's deadline, in the winter of 1932–33. If it didn't, the river would rise again and there wouldn't be another opportunity until the next winter, in 1933–34, after the deadline had passed. In fact, for Six Companies, building Hoover Dam successfully depended on this: Turn the river in the winter of 1932, and the whole project would immediately be almost a year ahead of schedule. Miss the chance, and the project would fall behind before construction of the main dam even began. The penalties would pile up, and the profit Six Companies hoped to make would start to drain away.

The fastest way to build the diversion tunnels was not to start at one end and dig toward the other. Instead, Six Companies began work in the middle, then at both ends. In May 1931, almost as soon as work started in Black Canyon, crews had started excavating access tunnels called adits. They burrowed into the canyon wall until they reached the planned course of the diversion tunnels about halfway along their length. Then they turned north and south and began excavating the first part of the main tunnels in both directions, a twelve-foot square section called a pioneer tunnel. This pioneer tunnel would be enlarged to create the diversion tunnel's fifty-six-foot diameter. To get tools and equipment to where they were needed and to haul away the excavated rock—the muck—workers laid narrow-gauge railroad tracks in the pioneer tunnels and adits. Miniature railroad cars and electric-powered locomotives were floated down the river on barges and hoisted into the adit entrances.

Miners working in a pioneer tunnel with a small mucking machine that ran on rails, September 1931.

As soon as roads were built into the canyon and more men and bigger machines could be moved into position, work began on driving and enlarging the tunnels from the ends. The first blast shook the canyon on September 17, two thousand feet downriver from the damsite at the bottom opening, or portal, of Tunnel 4. Work at the top and bottom portals of the other three tunnels began soon after. By December, when Marion started work, twelve hundred men were employed drilling, blasting, and excavating from the ends and from the middle of each of the tunnels. Eight 100-ton power shovels and a hundred dump trucks were kept busy hauling away the muck. "Neither the sizzling summer heat nor the advent of legal holidays was allowed to slow things up," reported a construction industry magazine.

The lower entrance to Tunnel 4 on September 25, a week after blasting started. Part of a white circle surveyors painted on the canyon wall to show the tunnel location is still visible.

The miners worked twenty-four hours a day, seven days a week, in three shifts. First, a team of drillers used big water-cooled compressed-air drills called liners to bore holes into the rock. Explosives were inserted into the boreholes, tapped carefully into place with long wooden rods, and connected to a four-hundred-volt electrical circuit. Then the tunnel was cleared and a switch thrown to detonate the explosives. A bulldozer moved in and piled up the blasted rock, and a power shovel loaded it into dump trucks to be taken away. Then the drillers stepped up to the rock face again and the process was repeated—foot by foot, hour after hour, day after day. "No one working for Six Companies had any days off," said a dam worker. "They worked straight through."

Approaching the work for the first time, Marion Allen heard a deafening roar and saw a giant steel-and-timber contraption on wheels, illuminated by bright floodlights—a "monstrosity about three stories high and covered with pipes and what looked like jackhammers, except that they were bigger," he remembered.

December 1931: A drilling jumbo backed up to the rock face. The pioneer tunnel is at top right.

This monstrosity was a drilling jumbo, built by Six Companies to speed up work. It consisted of a multilevel work platform built on the back of a dismantled truck and plumbed with water pipes and air hoses for the liners. It looked like it was made from scrap and might tip over at any moment, but it saved a lot of time. Each round of blasting for the main sections of the tunnels required drilling almost a hundred boreholes in a rock face forty feet high and more than fifty feet wide. Instead of building and dismantling temporary scaffolding for the miners to stand on between every round, the jumbo could be driven into position against the rock face for drilling, then moved out of the way for blasting and mucking out—and back into place for the next round.

The roar came from the thirty liners mounted on the jumbo, driving drill bits as much as twenty feet long into hard rock. "We could feel the vibration, as well as hear the noise, and with the bright floodlights the jumbo seemed to be floating," said Marion. Talk was impossible, so the drill operators used hand signals to ask for fresh steel (drill bits) and other tools: four fingers for "fetch me an eight-foot drill bit," five fingers for a ten-foot bit, and so on. Work went on without pause—with seemingly little regard for safety. A short while into Marion's shift, a truck loaded with explosives raced up to the jobsite—"going pretty fast," he remembered—and the driver started throwing boxes of charges to the crew. One man missed his catch and the box hit the ground and burst, scattering sticks of dynamite in the dirt.

Marion quickly got used to the pace and the din and learned what was expected of him, but on that first day it was overwhelming. "After watching it in the glaring light and noise I seemed to be going to sleep or felt I was being hypnotized," he remembered. When his shift ended at midnight, he made his way across a footbridge to the other side of the river for a ride back to Boulder City. The never-ending stream of trucks and men continued around him. "I was half way to Boulder City before my ears quit ringing," he said.

"It took a little while to fill up those empty bellies"

"When your shift was up, everyone tried to get to the little trucks first so you'd get home quicker," said dam worker Saul Wixson. To ferry workers between Boulder City and the construction site, Six Companies operated a fleet of transport trucks. For those who didn't find a seat on one of the smaller, faster trucks, the alternative was a ride on one of the lumbering double-deckers, nicknamed Big Berthas. The Big Berthas could take an hour or more to make the trip—and the men didn't completely trust them. One of the drivers told Marion Allen that his knees always shook as he climbed the steep grade out of the canyon. "He knew if he missed a gear it was doubtful the brakes would hold and there was nowhere to go but straight down!"

"Home" for many of the workers was a seven-by-ten-foot room with an iron bed, a mattress, and a chair in one of the new Six Companies dormitories in Boulder City. Each room had a window, electric light, and air coolers. Each building had a shower block, watercoolers, porches for sleeping or sitting outside, a janitor, and a regular supply of clean sheets

Workers boarding transport trucks outside a dormitory in Boulder City, November 1931.

and pillowcases. The rooms were small, simple, and cheaply built, but they were an improvement over the suffocating, pest-infested conditions at River Camp and the tents in Ragtown.

Across the street from the dormitories was the mess hall: two dining rooms that could each seat six hundred people, connected by an industrial-size kitchen that had its own bakery and butcher's shop and ran a 160-acre farm to supply butter, cream, and milk. Six Companies hired a catering company, Anderson Brothers, which had previously catered to movie studios in Hollywood, to operate the kitchen and mess hall.

To feed men working different shifts, the mess served breakfast, dinner, and supper twice a day each and provided lunches for men to take to work. Across much of the United States people were unemployed and hungry, but for workers at Hoover Dam there was plenty of food. "You could eat as long as you could eat, and they'd keep bringing it to you," said Bob Parker. "That went over big with these people who had been in breadlines. It took a little while to fill up those empty bellies."

"That was very interesting," remembered Tommy Nelson, "how these guys could get as many as ten or twelve sandwiches into a lunch box that probably was ten inches square by four inches deep...maybe a couple pieces of pie, an apple, and an orange. They loaded 'em up."

A wing of the mess hall in Boulder City set for a meal, September 1931.

After a slow start and the trouble at River Camp, Six Companies tackled housing and feeding the workforce with the same single-minded efficiency that it tackled building the dam. Six months earlier, Boulder City had been empty desert. By November 1931, the company had built five dormitories with 172 rooms each for single men, and more than a hundred three-room cottages for families. It spent more than $800,000 on housing and other facilities in the first year of construction. Meanwhile, streets and sidewalks and a public water supply and sewer system were being built by the government.

Six Companies' approach was practical. "We must have a place to eat and sleep before we can put men out there," said Frank Crowe—and work would have been impossible "out there" in such extreme conditions without a place to recover.

It was also progressive—meaning, it was forward-looking and considered the welfare of its employees. Single rooms, showers, and professionally cooked meals were almost unheard of on construction camps in the 1930s, where shelter was more likely to be a tent or a rough shack and the same cheap and unappetizing food was served day after day. Along with the dormitories and the mess hall, Six Companies also built a modern thirty-five-bed hospital in Boulder City and provided health insurance for its employees—another progressive innovation at the time.

"Something new had entered the American scene on the heels of the great depression—social consciousness," wrote a visitor. The United States government knew the country was watching what was happening at Hoover Dam and saw it as an opportunity to set a standard for living conditions for working people during the Great Depression. "The

Boulder Canyon Project...has aroused the interest of the people of the United States to a greater degree than any other project of the Government," it said. The government planned Boulder City as a model town: It hired a landscape architect to lay out the streets and public spaces and a town manager to oversee its operation. The town manager had almost complete power to decide who could live there, how many and what types of businesses could open, how the law was enforced, even how people maintained their property. "In a sense, the Hoover Dam project is not only a construction job but also a sociological venture," reported a magazine, approvingly.

But the facilities provided for the workforce weren't free. Along with being practical and progressive, they were operated to make a profit. A room, meals, and transport to and from work cost workers $1.60 a day—for the lowest-paid, making around $4 a day, almost half their wages. Health insurance cost them $1.50 per month. The dormitories and mess hall, as well as the buses, laundry, a recreation hall, and a department store, were all run by the Boulder City Company—which was, in reality, Six Companies operating under a different name. Charges for room and meals were deducted from the men's paychecks, which reduced the amount of cash the company had to pay out on paydays, and the profits added to its earnings.

Some saw an imbalance of power between men working seven days a week in an isolated desert settlement and Six Companies, which managed the supply and sold them most of what they needed. But there weren't many complaints. The men had a steady paycheck, and when they arrived at work, they were rested and well-fed. Marion Allen said, "I think one of the reasons the construction work on Hoover Dam went so well, even under such adverse conditions as the terrific heat which never let up day or night until late fall, the floods, slides, and falling rocks—all were coped with because after a shift was over we went back to Boulder City where we were able to relax and forget the job."

Racing the clock to turn the river, Frank Crowe and Six Companies understood what this meant: more work per shift.

"You had to be dead, absolutely dead"

In Black Canyon, the tunnels crept forward, faster and farther each month: sixty feet in September, six hundred feet in October, more than six thousand feet in January. Tunneling crews competed to see which could make the most progress. "You had to beat the other crew," said Marion Allen. "You had to get more footage. 'We got two more feet than you did!' This was the whole conversation."

"Records Are Smashed," reported the *Las Vegas Age* on January 27, 1932. "A new record was made last Wednesday when 256 linear feet of the big 41 by 56 foot tunnels were excavated in a single 24-hour shift." Two hundred fifty-six feet in a day—about the length of a city block—required blasting and removing sixteen thousand cubic yards of dirt and rock—well over a thousand truckloads.

As fast as the crews worked, the Colorado River could still stop them in their tracks. In September and January flash floods halted work, and in February twelve hundred workers were temporarily laid off and tunneling halted for a week when the river rose more than sixteen feet above its normal level, bursting into the tunnels and washing away a bridge. The flood left tools and machines crusted with mud, and the water left in the tunnels was so full of silt that it clogged mechanical pumps. It had to be shoveled out, or left to dry and harden, to be drilled and blasted away later. "On the first shift we were back we worked in water—really mud—up to our waists," said Marion Allen. "It was typical Colorado water—too thick to pump."

Cleaning up after floods inundated the tunnels and construction site in February 1932.

As the tunnels got deeper and farther from fresh air, the temperature rose, and the atmosphere inside could become suffocating—even deadly. Each round of blasting left behind a cloud of dust and dynamite smoke. It was usual for miners to wait between fifteen and thirty minutes after a blast for the air to clear before going back to work, but Six Companies crews—racing one another and racing to finish the job—returned to work in as little as five minutes. The company didn't discourage them. "Tests showed that, under working conditions, activities could be resumed in five minutes with perfect safety and comfort," it claimed.

But more dangerous than the blasting fumes was carbon monoxide gas in the exhaust from the gasoline-powered trucks and bulldozers mucking out the tunnels. Carbon monoxide is poisonous: It causes headaches, dizziness, and vomiting and can lead to loss of consciousness, brain damage, and death. Most dangerous, it is invisible and has no smell—so the damage could be done before workers knew gas was in the air.

Six Companies planned to use the same fleet of gas-powered trucks through all phases of the construction of the dam and did not want to spend money on a second fleet of electric trucks designed specially for use underground. It claimed that natural air currents, the use of fans, and the ventilation provided by the pioneer tunnels "maintained a cool, clean, and pleasant working condition" and that carbon monoxide pollution was "insignificant in comparison to that of vehicular tunnels."

Many workers disagreed. "Driving trucks through these tunnels, there was a gas problem there, real bad at times," said Curley Francis. "We usually could tell by looking at the lights in the tunnel. If they had a

Gasoline-powered trucks lined up at the entrance to a diversion tunnel, January 1932. The trucks' exhaust could cause poisonous carbon monoxide gas to build up in the tunnels.

blue ring around them, we would know the gas was getting pretty rough in there."

John Gieck remembered going to work one night in a crew of seventeen men. In the morning, he was one of just four left—the rest had been taken out sick. "You look down that tunnel and them lights was yellow," he said. "It was rough."

Nevada mining laws prohibited the use of gas-powered machinery underground, and in November the state ordered Six Companies to stop.

Six Companies responded with a lawsuit challenging the law and the state's authority to enforce it. A hearing was scheduled for early in 1932.

Meanwhile, the company continued using the gas-powered trucks, and workers taken to the Boulder City hospital with symptoms were diagnosed with pneumonia, heart disease, and similar conditions—never carbon monoxide poisoning. "They never had that," said Joe Kine. "They all died with pneumonia if they made it to the hospital." Between September 1931, when the trucks began work in the tunnels, and the end of the year, five workers were recorded as having died from pneumonia and one from heart disease in the Boulder City hospital, but none from carbon monoxide poisoning. In fact, not a single death from carbon monoxide was recorded during the five years it took to build Hoover Dam. But more than forty dam workers were recorded as having died from pneumonia, while not one person from the rest of the population of Boulder City died from pneumonia during the same period.

With no recorded cases of carbon monoxide poisoning, Six Companies could argue that work in the tunnels was safe. It also meant no compensation. Death from pneumonia was considered a "natural cause," not a workplace accident. "If you said they died of gases in the tunnels, they were obligated to compensate you, to compensate the family," remembered Mary Eaton, whose husband worked for Six Companies. "So they'd just say pneumonia, and they'd get by with that. We never felt that was fair."

Or as another worker put it: "You had to be dead, absolutely dead, down on the job to get killed on the job. If they ever got you in the hospital, you didn't get killed on the job, you just died....It's just bad luck."

The dispute between the state of Nevada and Six Companies was decided in April. Six Companies had argued that because Hoover Dam was being built on federal land, the state did not have authority to enforce its laws there; that converting its trucks from gas to electric power would cost too much and delay work; and that the tunnels were properly ventilated and safe. The court ruled in favor of Six Companies—but by then it wouldn't have mattered if the company had lost. In the time it had taken for the court to reach a decision, excavation of the diversion tunnels was all but finished. Most of the gas-powered trucks were back aboveground, and Six Companies was one step closer to turning the river.

"By dawn the riverbed was dry"

At 10:00 p.m. on Sunday, January 31, 1932, the crew working upstream from the bottom of Tunnel 3 on the Arizona side of the Colorado blasted away the last few feet of rock and broke through to meet the upper section, coming from the top. Tunnel 2, on the Nevada side, was holed through five days later. By May, all four tunnels had been opened from end to end.

But they weren't finished. After the main sections were holed through, crews followed blasting and drilling out the semicircular floor section— called the invert—and trimming away rock in the walls and roof until what remained was a circle fifty-six feet in diameter. Then the circle was lined with three feet of concrete, turning the rough rock tunnel into a smooth, round pipeline, fifty feet in diameter.

Lining the tunnels with concrete required another kind of jumbo—a giant wheeled contraption like the drilling jumbo that could be rolled up and down the tunnels to where it was needed. These finishing jumbos ran on rails and carried curved molds, or forms, the shape of the finished tunnel. The concrete was poured behind them, in between the form and rock—first the invert, then the sidewalls, then the roof. Men in boots climbed down into the invert, or in between the sidewall forms and the walls, and puddled the concrete, stomping and shoveling it into place to make sure that it was evenly mixed and that there were no air pockets. Overhead, the concrete was blown into the space between the roof and the form by compressed-air concrete guns. The jumbo and the forms

A crew getting ready to pour concrete in the invert of one of the diversion tunnels. Behind them, a poured section of the floor is drying, and in the background a sidewall jumbo with semicircular forms is in position to pour the walls.

were left in place until the concrete hardened, or cured, then moved forward to begin the next section.

It was dirty work. "When we came home from work down there, we didn't hang our clothes up; we stood 'em up," said Tommy Nelson.

And it was hot. "The ones you felt sorry for were the ones that had to get in the forms and puddle the concrete," said another worker, Carl Merrill. "It was extremely warm. Concrete is normally hot. And it was extremely warm back there."

A forty-foot section of sidewall took about two days to finish: twenty-four hours to pour and puddle the concrete, ten hours for it to cure, plus time to set up and remove the forms. Concrete work began in March and went on steadily through the spring and summer of 1932. At the beginning of November the linings of the two tunnels on the Arizona side of the river were finished.

That same week, on November 8, elections were held in the United States, and the country voted overwhelmingly to elect a new president, Franklin Roosevelt. Four days later, the defeated president, Herbert Hoover, took a detour to visit the damsite on his way back to Washington, DC, from his home in California. With his wife, Lou, he was driven through one of the diversion tunnels by Walker Young, then to a viewpoint overlooking the canyon. They visited the mess hall in Boulder City during supper. Although he had championed the building of the dam, Hoover was widely blamed for the effects of the Great Depression, and residents of Boulder City had voted more than four to one for Roosevelt. "People were pretty bitter," said one worker who was present. "Some of the people even

President Hoover in one of the diversion tunnels at the damsite, November 12, 1932.

booed him....They wouldn't stand up. They kept on eating." Hoover made a short speech and left Boulder City after less than two hours.

If Hoover had stayed overnight, he could have witnessed a milestone in the construction of the dam that was named for him. "Diversion of Colorado Starts Today," announced the front page of the *Las Vegas Age* on November 13, next to its report on Hoover's visit. "The first major work on the mighty project will be completed when the waters of the river will be diverted through the newly completed bores," the paper wrote.

At 11:30 that morning, blasts demolished temporary earth dams in front of the entrances to Tunnels 3 and 4 on the Arizona side, allowing the river in for the first time. At the same time, a line of trucks began driving

November 14, 1932: Turning the river. Trucks dump rock into the Colorado, forcing it into two of the diversion tunnels. Downstream, below the bridge on the right, the river has slowed to a trickle.

onto a bridge over the river. Turning and backing up to the edge, they dumped loads of rock into the water.

"They were really excited about taking the river out of its channel because it's quite a task," remembered Bureau of Reclamation employee Steve Chubbs. "They had to have a lot of muck, and they had to have it handy, and they had to get it into the river fast, too."

"Fast" meant trucks kept coming—four per minute without interruption for the next thirty hours. "They worked all night. I forgot when they started, but I know by dawn the riverbed was dry," said Steve. In the early morning, the barrier built by truckload after truckload of rock began to break the surface of the water, and the river started to pool above it. The trucks continued dumping, and the barrier continued to grow, until around daybreak when the water flowing in Black Canyon slowed to a trickle and stopped, and the river turned instead into the new, man-made tunnels through the canyon walls. Eleven months ahead of schedule, the Colorado had been diverted.

"Everything had to be clean as one could imagine"

What remained in the riverbed when the river was gone was a hard-packed layer of rock, gravel, and silt as much as 140 feet deep, rolled and pounded into the bottom of Black Canyon over millions of years by the fierce Colorado. A dam couldn't be built on this stuff—it all had to be removed and the solid bedrock underneath exposed and scoured clean before construction could begin.

But first, the temporary cofferdams that would keep the river safely out of the canyon while the work went on had to be finished. One upstream from the damsite would keep the river diverted into the tunnels, even during the big summer floods, and one downstream would stop it

Black Canyon drying out, two weeks after the Colorado River was diverted.

from backing up into the construction site from below. Although they would be dwarfed and forgotten when Hoover Dam itself was built, these were dig dams: The upstream cofferdam was 98 feet high, 450 feet wide, and 750 feet thick at its base. It was built from rock and dirt, sealed along its edges with steel sheet and tire rubber, and paved with six inches of concrete. Work building this cofferdam had started even before the river was diverted, and by the end of December it was nearing completion.

"Year's End Sees Vast Amount of Work on Project Finished," reported the *Las Vegas Age* on Christmas Eve. Six Companies shut down work for an unusual two-day holiday and opened the construction site to visitors from Boulder City. Workers' families got to tour and drive their cars through one of the diversion tunnels. Back in town, children were invited to a free matinee at the new movie theater, and Santa Claus handed out candy and oranges.

The day after Christmas, work started again. Even though the project was almost a year ahead of schedule, Frank Crowe and the Six Companies engineers didn't slow down and didn't wait for one task to be finished before starting another. Before work on the main dam had begun, other parts of the system were under construction. Miners were digging almost thirty different tunnels for water pipes, access, and other purposes—one tunnel snaked 150 feet below the riverbed to a point right under the damsite, to serve as a drain and an inspection tunnel after the dam was built. Crews were excavating and finishing the spillways: two emergency overflow channels high on the canyon walls that would divert water if the reservoir ever got too high and threatened the dam.

One of the two spillways under construction in the spring of 1933.

Each was like a giant bathtub, 650 feet long, 150 feet wide, and 120 feet deep—big enough to hold a ship—with a drain at one end: a steep tunnel that plunged through the rock to connect to one of the diversion tunnels six hundred feet below. Just behind the damsite, rock platforms had been blasted out of the canyon walls and foundations started for the four tall intake towers that would draw water from the reservoir and feed it to the power plant.

In the smelly mud and rock that filled the riverbed, powdermen set explosives to loosen the debris. Hundreds of pipe fitters were kept busy installing and running pumps to remove the water that collected in pools in the bottom of the pit. An endless stream of trucks hauled the muck away. "Down below grunted and growled prehistoric monsters—great brute dinosaurs with massive bellies, with long necks like the brontosaurus, and with armored hides thick as those of the stegosaurus. They were

Excavation work in the bottom of Black Canyon in 1933. The Bureau of Reclamation took thousands of photographs to document and publicize the building of Hoover Dam. Its official photographer, Ben Glaha, took many of the most striking, including this one. "We want the world to know what is going on there and for that purpose, nothing is as effective as a good picture," wrote bureau commissioner Elwood Mead.

Wrecked trucks after an accident. Among the thousands of photographs taken during construction, almost none show accidents or injuries. The official photographs made by the Bureau of Reclamation emphasize industry, progress, and success. This photo was taken by a Six Companies photographer.

steam shovels and cranes feeding on the muck, a ton at a gulp," wrote a visitor. One day at the end of January, 1,841 truckloads were removed in a single eight-hour shift. Rumors circulated of gold nuggets being found, and the press reported that somebody had staked a mining claim near one of the Six Companies gravel pits. The report was published on April 1, but that didn't stop optimistic workers from panning through the dirt.

Like the riverbed, the abutments—where the walls of the canyon would meet the dam—had to be prepared before construction could begin. Hoover Dam was not attached to the rock by mechanical means, such as bolts, or chemical means, such as glue. It was held in place by gravity and the weight of the water in the reservoir pushing it against the canyon walls—so the rock had to be clean and smooth to make a good

High scalers at work on the abutment, January 1933.

seal. Equipped with jackhammers, pry bars, water jets, and explosives, high scalers spread out along the cliffs in wooden seats called bosun's chairs. The chairs hung from steel spikes driven into the rock above. "We dropped ourselves over," said Joe Kine. "We had good ropes. They didn't break. That was never any worry." When the ropes became frayed or worn, they were burned so no one could use them by mistake.

Following the directions of Bureau of Reclamation surveyors, the high scalers removed loose and protruding rock, scoured the surface, and shaped vertical notches in the walls high on each side of the canyon to create a keyway that would help anchor the dam structure. Tourists came to watch them at work, and stories were told about their fearlessness and daring. One high scaler was reported to have saved the life of a bureau engineer who slipped by swinging quickly through the air and wedging the man's body against the rock until help arrived. But stories of high scalers snatching falling bodies out of the air were exaggerated. "It couldn't possibly have happened," said Joe. "It would have broke a rope or something."

By the end of May 1933, crews working in the bottom of the canyon had reached the bedrock. Beneath the layers of compacted rock and gravel they found a deep V-shaped groove eroded in the middle of the riverbed. It was too narrow for the steam shovels and trucks to reach, and the last sections had to be excavated by hand. "It was slow work," said Curley Francis. "There was no machinery that could do that type of work."

(Opposite) Black Canyon a few days before construction of the dam began. The riverbed has been excavated and a railroad trestle built along the canyon wall to deliver concrete, while high scalers finish their work on the dam abutments.

It had been two years since the first crews had landed in Black Canyon. Now the Colorado was running through the diversion tunnels, the canyon bottom was empty and dry, and the walls were scoured smooth. It was "a beautiful sight to look at. It was actually stripped and washed and cleaned up," said Curley. "Everything had to be clean as one could imagine in order to start the concrete pouring."

CODA: WHITE WORKERS ONLY

Although Six Companies and the Bureau of Reclamation promoted its efforts as progressive, there was another reason for their determination to build comfortable housing and feed the workforce well. The construction contract required Six Companies to hire only American citizens. "American" was widely understood to mean "white." And it specifically prohibited the hiring of what it called "Mongolian" workers—meaning Asians (who at that time were also prohibited by law from becoming United States citizens).

Hoover Dam was the most visible construction project in the country and a centerpiece in the government's effort to put people to work during the Depression; it didn't want to face the disruption of its "American" workers collapsing or walking off the job in the desert heat, as they had during attempts to stop the Imperial Valley flood. "The government felt it desirable to limit the employment list as nearly as possible to white American citizens," said an article in the *New York Times Magazine*. "It has before it, thus, the task of keeping 3,000 or more Americans, mainly of the native and Northern European stocks, contented and healthy at hard labor jobs....Anything like a general health break-down among the 'help' would mean, of course, serious delay in the work and no doubt eventually the importation of foreign tropical labor."

The Bureau of Reclamation and Six Companies showed no embarrassment at the racism that characterized people of color as "foreign tropical labor." Instead they congratulated themselves on the lengths to which they were going to provide for their white workforce. An article in the trade publication *Compressed Air Magazine* spoke for Six Companies and the bureau. Using an offensive term for Asians that was commonplace at the time, it wrote: "Some prophesied that Orientals would finally have to be imported to cope with the melting temperatures that prevail in Black Canyon for four months of the year. To make certain nothing of this kind would happen, Uncle Sam decided to extend a kindly but firm paternal helping hand to the contractors and to set up a construction town under his control to insure for the workers a high standard of living and a maximum of comfort and general well-being."

Black Americans weren't explicitly prohibited from employment on the dam, but almost none were hired. They needed the jobs as much as whites—more so, in fact: Black men were twice as likely to be unemployed as white men during the Great Depression. When work started in 1931, no Black men were employed on the Hoover Dam project. In Las Vegas, the Black community formed the Colored Citizens Labor Protective Association to press the government for jobs, and the National

Black workers at the construction site in October 1932. Like the similar photograph of Indigenous workers opposite, this picture was apparently taken to highlight the men's ethnicity and record their employment on the project—there are no official photographs of groups of white workers posed this way.

Association for the Advancement of Colored People sent a representative to investigate and support their efforts. They pointed out that Black citizens had served in World War I and that the construction contract did require Six Companies to give preference to hiring veterans. After a meeting between Black leaders and officials of Six Companies and the Bureau of Reclamation in June 1932, Six Companies president Warren Bechtel claimed that he had "never heard of any refusal to employ

Indigenous workers employed as high scalers, October 1932.

colored people, but said he would take the matter up immediately on his return to Boulder City, and see that provision was made for their employment on the work when and if they had the necessary experience." Secretary of the Interior Ray Lyman Wilbur told the NAACP, "When additions to the force are made the company will arrange to give employment to negro labor."

Both Bechtel's stipulation that Black workers needed "experience" and Secretary Wilbur's statement that they would be hired "when additions to the force are made" were evasions: Hundreds of unskilled whites were hired; workers left the job and new ones were taken on almost daily. When ten Black men were hired soon after the meeting, it was little more than a gesture. In September there were twenty-five Blacks on Six Companies' payroll, and by the following summer about sixty-five—less than 2 percent of a workforce of around four thousand.

A group of Indigenous men was hired about the same time. "Six trained Apache Indians, high scalers, will perform in the dangerous reaches of Black Canyon on work being done on Hoover dam," reported the *Las Vegas Evening Review-Journal*. But the paper couldn't discard stereotypes about Indigenous Americans, calling them "sure-footed, brawny men" and writing, "Members of the tribe which followed the notorious Geronimo on his escapades, these men will now make war on the forces of nature with the white men."

Putting these men to work as high scalers also drew on stereotypes about Indigenous men not being afraid of heights. Meanwhile, many of the Black workers were assigned to work at gravel pits in the desert, where conditions were harshest, or given dirty work like scraping the rust off steel bars. They had to drink from segregated water buckets, traveled to and from Las Vegas in segregated buses, and were excluded from housing in Boulder City. "There wasn't any colored people in Boulder City," said Bob Parker. He remembered that when the owner of one of the cafés in town hired a Black cook, the town manager instructed him to fire the man. The café owner refused, but Boulder City was a white town. In fact, one of the explanations the Bureau of Reclamation gave for Black workers not being hired was that segregated housing would have to be provided for them: "The representatives of the Six Companies, Inc., have stated that while negroes would probably be desirable on account of the extreme heat," wrote a bureau official in 1931, "the matter of housing and segregation has so far rendered it impractical to plan on their employment."

The reality was that there were few opportunities for people of color to find work, that they faced discrimination in assignments, and that housing and other facilities were mostly closed to them. Hoover Dam was a white world.

Children in the yard of a Six Companies cottage. As the dam grew, so did Boulder City, becoming the third-largest town in Nevada. More than a construction camp for men, it was a community and a home for families whose lives had been uprooted by the Great Depression.

FOUR

A HOME IN
THE DESERT

"A gigantic but workaday job"

JUNE 6, 1933. THE SECOND PHASE OF THE CONSTRUCTION OF HOOVER Dam began with a bucket. It started its journey three-quarters of a mile upriver from the damsite in Black Canyon, at a mixing plant where it had been filled with eight cubic yards of carefully measured and tested concrete. A train carried the bucket to the site, where a hook dropped from a cable overhead and lifted it over the canyon. "Swinging far out over the center of the great pit, the load came swiftly and silently down to repose gently on the very bottom of the excavation," reported the *Las Vegas Age*. There, C. W. Bingham, "a veteran dam workman," unhooked safety catches on the bottom of the bucket with his shovel, stood back, and dumped the first load of concrete on Hoover Dam.

Another bucket followed, and another and another—the first in a constant stream that would continue around the clock for the next twenty

The first bucket of concrete poured on Hoover Dam, June 6, 1933.

months. With the river flowing through the tunnels and the high scalers' work mostly finished, the most dramatic and dangerous work on the dam was done. What remained was methodically building a vast concrete wall across Black Canyon: "Just a gigantic but workaday job," the *Las Vegas Evening Review-Journal* called it.

The dam wasn't built in one solid mass, but in a patchwork of dozens of separate columns. The columns were built side by side, and then the gaps between them were filled in. They rose in layers, five feet at a time. Fence-like wooden forms were built around the tops of the columns; concrete was poured into the forms and allowed to cure; then the forms were raised and another layer was poured on top. As the dam grew it looked like a stack of children's building blocks scattered in the canyon.

It took a huge amount of concrete: roughly 3.4 million cubic yards by the time the dam was finished. The concrete came fast—an average of nearly seven hundred buckets a day—and it had to be delivered and poured before it hardened, in temperatures that ranged from over 100 degrees in summer to below freezing in winter. Not only that, but Frank Crowe had estimated that Six Companies could pour concrete more cheaply than anyone else—more cheaply than even the government thought possible, in fact. Six Companies' profits depended on making the concrete and moving it to where it was needed without wasting a

September 1933: Three months after the first bucket of concrete was poured, Hoover Dam is a patchwork of concrete columns rising in Black Canyon. Each column has a wooden form at the top. The railroad trestle and a train carrying concrete buckets clings to the canyon wall at right.

moment. Doing so required a different system of transportation from the excavating and mucking in the tunnels and the riverbed. "The rumble of a great fleet of the largest trucks ever built...is stilled," continued the *Age*'s report. In its place came the rattle of trains running on tracks along the canyon walls, and the hum of a system of moving cableways that crisscrossed the sky above.

The mixing plant upriver from the cofferdam was called Lo-Mix because it was "low down" in the canyon, at river level. There, it was close to a supply of one ingredient needed to make concrete: water. The other ingredients were cement and an aggregate of rock, gravel, and sand. The cement was hauled down from the yards in Boulder City. Gravel was dug from pits ten miles away, across the river in Arizona, and sorted and graded with other aggregate at a site in the desert north of Black Canyon. Everything was moved by rail: Six Companies built and operated its own railroad connecting Boulder City, the worksite, the sorting yard, and the gravel pits. Keeping the dam supplied with concrete required an average of 25 train cars of cement and 150 of aggregate to be delivered to the mixing plants every day. Thirteen locomotives and more than 120 cars ran on twenty miles of track, with a staff of seventy engineers, crew, and other operators.

The railroad was said to be the busiest in the western United States at the time, and the last mile, from Lo-Mix to the damsite, to have been the most expensive to build. It ran along a track bed dynamited out of the vertical canyon walls, through a thousand-foot tunnel, and ended on a trestle clinging precariously to the rock face two hundred feet above the riverbed, supported by long steel legs. At the company machine shops, mechanics converted the miniature electric locomotives that had been used for mucking out the pioneer tunnels to run on the line, and built special flatbed cars to hold the concrete buckets. Each car had space for four of them, exactly spaced so that they would line up underneath the mixing machines at Lo-Mix for loading.

Train cars left Lo-Mix with two full buckets of concrete and two empty spaces. When they arrived at the trestle above the construction site, a hoist hook suspended from an overhead cableway swooped out of the canyon carrying an empty bucket, dropped it into a space on the train car, picked up a full bucket, and swooped away again. The train inched forward, the process was repeated, and when the full buckets had been switched for empties it shuttled back down the line to Lo-Mix for another load.

The overhead cableways could deliver a bucket of concrete—or a machine, a load of timber or steel, or a section of pipe—to the site below in a matter of moments. Five construction cableways crossed the canyon above the dam. A hoist car with a hook ran along each, with the cable ends attached to towers that ran along the canyon rim on railroad tracks. The hook could be raised up and down, the hoist car moved from side to side, and the towers back and forward, meaning a load could be maneuvered to reach any point in the three-dimensional space below. Along with the concrete and construction supplies, the cableways also delivered men. Crowded into an open wooden basket called a skip, workers were ferried from one side of the canyon to the other or from the rim down to the riverbed—a three-minute plunge through the air that saved a thirty-minute trip by road. Sometimes the skips and cableways were used to pluck high scalers off the canyon walls and move them to a new worksite.

Like the tunneling, pouring concrete went on around the clock. Banks of floodlights lit up the site at night. As the dam spread across Black Canyon and the columns grew, the pace increased: more concrete, more trains, and more pressure on the operators to keep them moving. "It was kind of interesting in that particular time, too, that as the dam started to grow, the cableways became more demanding....You had to haul concrete faster all the time," said Curley Francis, who had exchanged his job driving a truck for one driving a train. A second set of railroad tracks and a second mixing plant, called Hi-Mix, were built high up on the canyon rim to deliver concrete from above. Curley remembered that there could be as many as nine concrete trains running at once and that he and the other drivers relied on the switch operator to prevent them from crashing into one another. "This was a mass confusion," he said. "You'd be looking down the track and see another train coming right for you; then all of a sudden they'd switch him around you, and as soon as he went by, you'd go on by."

Sometimes the operator got overwhelmed. "They had a large whistle on top of that switch tower, and anytime that man hung onto that whistle, everybody stopped, because we all knew he was confused and didn't know where everybody was at." Once, it got to be too much altogether: "All of a sudden he just pulled all the switches like that and blew the whistle and walked out. He couldn't stand it any longer," Curley remembered.

(Opposite) An overhead cableway delivers workers from the rim to the canyon bottom in an open wooden skip.

A Six Companies train delivers a load of cement and aggregate on the narrow, crowded railroad on the canyon rim.

"It was an amazement to me that we didn't have more wrecks than we did," he said.

Once the machines had delivered the concrete to the top of a column, it was the work of men to finish the pour by hand. Wearing rubber boots and armed with shovels and leveling tools, they stomped and shoveled the wet concrete into place, making sure it was evenly mixed and spread into every corner of the forms. They set pipes, drains, and instruments such as thermometers in place, and shaped inspection

At the top of one of the dozens of columns making the dam's structure, a work crew empties a bucket of concrete into a wooden form.

passageways and elevator shafts that would run inside the finished dam. Every pour on every column had to be checked and approved by a Bureau of Reclamation inspector. Then, after the concrete had set, it was scoured with high-pressure water and air jets to leave a clean, rough surface. A thin, one-inch layer of grout—a mixture of cement, sand, and water—was spread to form a bond, and a layer of fresh concrete poured on top.

With concrete being poured day and night, the massive columns spreading across and upward—and with work continuing on the pipelines, spillways, and intake towers around the main dam—the workforce grew. Nearby Boulder City grew as well, to a population of over six thousand, making it the third-biggest town in Nevada. Along with the Six Companies shift workers traveling to and from the site every eight hours, there were other contractors making pipe and machinery that would be installed on the dam, government engineers supervising its construction and planning its operation, and people building and opening businesses.

Many of them had families. The government paved the streets of Boulder City, built a water and sewer system, and employed a police force and a landscaper, and engineers working for the Bureau of Reclamation even built themselves a golf course. But it hadn't made plans for families—"apparently feeling it would be man's town," a reporter said. "But it wasn't." With families came children, and with children came the need for schools and other resources.

"That was the start of the little schoolhouse out in the desert"

"Of course, with the building of the dam being the center of our lives, it was the center of the children's lives, and they built dams all over the backyard," remembered Lillian Whalen, who lived in Boulder City. For construction equipment the kids raided the pantry: "They snitched their mothers' tablespoons and teaspoons to dig in the soft sand, so some of us had silver-plated backyards," she said.

For Lillian and many families, home in Boulder City was a Six Companies cottage. The company built more than 660 of them, in addition to the dormitories it built for single workers: quickly constructed, identical wooden houses laid out in straight lines in the desert—like shoeboxes sitting on sand, said one woman who lived there. The parts were precut and delivered like a kit, and a crew of two carpenters could assemble one of them in about twelve hours. They had two or three rooms, a porch, a toilet and shower, a gas stove, and electric light, but no furniture. People brought what they had, and scrounged scrap lumber from around town to make closets and other things they needed. The Boulder City Company rented the houses to the dam workers: $19 a month for a two-room cottage, $30 a month for a three-room cottage.

"You think you can put a house up in one day and have it look like anything?" said another resident, Wilma Cooper. "They never were comfortable, because there was no insulation in 'em. And the sheetrock inside was so thin—you sneeze on it, you'd blow a hole in it." The houses

Like shoeboxes sitting on sand: Six Companies cottages
under construction in Boulder City, June 1931.

were cold in winter, when people used small kerosene stoves for heat,
and sweltering in summer. For air-conditioning they blew a fan over a
burlap sack hung in a window, which they kept wet with a trickle of water from a hose. The houses were drafty all year long. Windblown sand
found its way in through cracks in the walls and the floorboards and had
to be swept out all the time. It settled on people while they slept. "You
always flopped over and turned your head down before you opened your
eyes in the morning, or you'd get sand in them," said Wilma.

The blowing sand and identical houses and streets made it easy to
get lost. Helen Holmes remembered losing her way to the outhouse
before plumbing was installed in her cottage. Children got lost playing
outside—"they didn't dare get out of your sight because they didn't know
where their home was," said Helen. Sometimes workers coming home
in the dark got lost and ended up walking into the wrong cottage. To try

and keep the sand under control—as well as provide some shade and make Boulder City look less barren and bleak—the Boulder City Company gave tenants who put in lawns and planted their yards a discount on their water utility bills, and the Bureau of Reclamation hired a landscaper to plant trees and lawns in the town's public spaces. But as fast as the gardeners planted the lawns, the sand blew back and buried them. Some sandstorms left behind drifts a foot deep that had to be shoveled off the new grass.

But for families who had been living in a tent, or who had lost everything in the Depression, the shoebox houses and the sandy yards were a new beginning. People began moving from Ragtown and other campsites in the late summer of 1931, and they kept arriving—as many as eight new cottages and eight new families a day. As fast as the cottages went up, there was always a shortage and a list of families waiting for one—"always a big line up of people begging for houses, and applications for houses," said Rose Lawson. Rose remembered how much it meant to have running water and a shower: "I jumped out of bed and then took a shower before I even thought of starting breakfast. Then in the afternoon you'd have another shower. Then when you got ready to go to bed, you'd have another shower," she said. "I think those showers were about the most precious things in Boulder City."

As well as a house with plumbing and electricity, people moving to Boulder City found new shops and other businesses. At first, there was just the Boulder City Company Stores, which opened in the fall of 1931. It sold fresh vegetables, meat, and groceries as well as clothes, hardware, drugs, and appliances such as iceboxes and stoves—"a complete shopping center," declared the store's advertisements. But by the following spring, there were two dozen more businesses in town. In March the *Boulder City Journal* ran a special edition celebrating the town's first anniversary and its "miraculous" growth in just a year. An ad for the city's businesses in the *Las Vegas Age* listed a doctor, two dentists, a chiropractor, an optometrist, two beauty parlors, a barbershop, and a music teacher. There was a second department store, a lumber yard, a hardware store, drugstores, a business that made and sold ice, and several cafés offering an alternative to the Six Companies mess hall. In May, a theater opened, with shows in the morning, afternoon, and evening so workers coming

Clothing and shoe department in the Boulder City Company Stores, June 1932.

off all three shifts could catch a movie, and air-conditioning so they could escape the heat. Baseball and other sports leagues got started: "Accountants Beat Engineers at Ball," read a May headline in the *Journal*, which also reported that there were so many teams that a second league was needed.

At first, houses in Boulder City were built and owned by either the Bureau of Reclamation or Six Companies. But as soon as the bureau started leasing plots of land to others, people were quick to begin building homes of their own. Erma Godbey and her husband, Tom, were among the first. "We were trying to get away from it," said Erma, "and get into a civilized type of living as fast as we possibly could." In the summer of 1932, they signed the lease for a building lot. Erma sketched a plan on a piece of scrap paper, and they borrowed, scrounged, and bartered for the materials and labor they needed. The lumber came from a disused building belonging to a contractor that had put up electrical transmission wires, doors from a church that didn't need them, and cabinets and counters for the kitchen from the town's first police station. Erma remembered that they still had a map drawn on them showing directions to a bootlegger's camp in the desert that the police had raided.

Erma and Tom's fifth child, Alice, was born in the house soon after they built it. Six Companies employees and their families could use the company hospital in Boulder City, but others like Erma had a choice between traveling to the hospital in Las Vegas or having their babies at home. According to Lillian Whalen, town doctor John McDaniel "delivered many of them on the screen porches of the little houses, with fans drifting around." But, she added, "it was a healthy thing, because he never lost a mother or a baby."

Growing families created a predicament for the government. More than half of the men working for Six Companies were married. Some couples had children already, and almost all of them were young, so soon they had more: An estimated 200 babies were born in Boulder City in 1931; 220 in 1932; and 340 in 1933. The town was said to have the highest birth rate in the country at the time.

The state of Nevada—which didn't collect taxes in Boulder City because it was federal property—didn't provide schools there. So when the beginning of the school year came around in the fall of 1931, the first schools in the town were started by parents. Families still living in Ragtown set up a classroom in a disused storage building. In Boulder City, Zella Larson ran a school for first and second graders in her home. Outside of town, near the railroad junction called the "Y," Charles Elder built a schoolhouse from donated lumber. "One day here came a big, big load of lumber," remembered Velma Holland. "The men around, they got their hammers and their saws and went over and helped him." They built a classroom, desks, and benches, and put up a chalkboard made of black construction tar paper. Finally, said Velma, "they got ahold of a one-by-two or something, and nailed it up, and put a flag on it, and that was the start of the little schoolhouse out in the desert."

The teachers were volunteers, most of them mothers who had been teachers before moving to Boulder City, and the schools charged a fee to cover expenses, $1.50 per week. Six Companies gave them the use of three new cottages for schoolhouses. The company also built a

The little schoolhouse out in the desert: Children outside their home-built school near the railroad "Y."

playground, and the company store donated desks and chairs and provided stoves and fuel.

But the number of children quickly outgrew the volunteer schools. "The many new families moving into the city have resulted in overtaxing school accommodations and the problem is said to be acute," reported the *Las Vegas Age* in December, three months into the school year. At the beginning of 1932, the Bureau of Reclamation asked Congress for funds for a school. Congress agreed—but only to pay for the building, not the teachers. As more than 80 percent of the children belonged to the families of men working for Six Companies, the company was persuaded to provide the money for teachers' salaries.

Eleven women of "outstanding ability" were hired, wrote the town manager, and on the morning of September 26, the new public school in

Boulder City opened its doors to almost 550 elementary school students, "while two special police officers patrolled the street crossings in an effort to reduce possibilities of accidents." Two weeks later, high school opened in the building with 109 students and three more teachers, paid for by another contractor, Babcock & Wilcox, which had won the contract to make the steel pipes for the dam.

There was no kindergarten at the public school, and high school seniors still had to travel to Las Vegas for classes. The Bureau of Reclamation didn't have money for a kindergarten teacher, or for a science lab and other facilities for twelfth grade. But just a year and a half after the first families arrived in Ragtown and the other camps in the desert, Boulder City had its first public school.

A year after the first, temporary schoolhouses were built, elementary school students have a new school building in Boulder City, October 1932.

"We came here and there was none of that"

Most of the women who got teaching jobs at the new school in Boulder City had one particular qualification: They were single.

What women did in Boulder City—and in America in the 1930s—was shaped by custom and by the economy. Unmarried women could find work. Married women whose husbands were employed generally could not. It was accepted that a family needed only one income, and with jobs scarce during the Depression, many employers made it a rule. Edna French, who lived in Boulder City after she was married, explained: "I had been a home ec teacher, and I tried to get into the schools in Vegas. But they had a policy—which they followed in Boulder City, too—that there should be only one breadwinner in the family."

The practice was known as the marriage bar. Lucille Finney encountered it when she got married. She had been the first woman employed in Boulder City, working at the town's post office when it opened in a makeshift building in the spring of 1931; then she went to work for Six Companies. The *Boulder City Journal* announced her engagement in May 1932, reporting that she had "resigned her position in the accounting office of Six Companies."

Unmarried or otherwise, no women were employed in construction, and the damsite in Black Canyon was restricted to men. Only one woman went there regularly—a newspaper reporter, Florence Lee Jones. Florence graduated from the University of Missouri with a degree in journalism.

Boulder City's first public elementary school teachers, October 1932. Front row: Principal Leila Tilley, Ruth Chadburn, Florence Smith, and Alice Marie Connoly. Middle row: Margaret Hunt, Therese Winston, Audrey Reber, and Carol Beecher. Back row: Lyla Campbell Duffy, Harriet Gossett, and Florence Gustin.

Her father ran a gas station near Boulder City, and while her brothers paid their way through college by working on the dam, she found a job with the *Las Vegas Evening Review-Journal*. There were few jobs for reporters at the time, and even fewer for women. "Only three in our class of 100 went into journalism," she said. "Men were store clerks and gas station attendants. Those were the only jobs they could find." Florence was assigned to visit the damsite twice a week. She "knew all the foremen down there and a lot of the workers. She was just one of the gang," said her editor. "She could go anywhere on the dam anytime, day or night, and would be admitted to any part of the project." She was also the Las Vegas correspondent for the Associated Press news service, so many of her stories about Hoover Dam appeared in papers around the country.

Six Companies and the Bureau of Reclamation hired women as office staff, but they were relatively few. With the headline "Women Also Play Part in Building Huge Hoover Dam," the *Las Vegas Age* reported that women were employed taking dictation, answering phones, and doing clerical work for the government—but the paper struggled to make a story out of it. "The number of women is only five," it admitted, "but all are employed in important positions, according to bureau officials."

Alice Hamilton made $125 a month working for Six Companies, as secretary for its security chief. She remembered that two other women worked in the company office and that Frank Crowe's secretary was a man. Alice's story was unusual because she was married. She was able to continue working and helped catalog and sell equipment the company no longer needed after construction was finished. But Alice was never able to rent a company cottage because even though she worked for Six Companies, her husband did not. "I would always be bottom of the list," she said.

Most women who came to Boulder City looked for opportunity and a way to make a living away from the construction site. It wasn't easy, and with so many unemployed they had to compete with men for jobs. "There weren't very many jobs for women in town," said Dorothy Nunley. Besides teaching and clerical work, they worked in cafés and stores, in childcare, and in service businesses like laundry. Dorothy tried working as a waitress, then as help for a woman with seven children for $3 a week, then she went to work at the Boulder City Company laundry, pressing sheets and shirts for $16 a week—"until I got married," she added.

Some women started businesses. Ida Browder had worked in a restaurant in Salt Lake City, and after her husband died she moved to Boulder City with her two children to open one there. There were no buildings to rent in the new town. People starting businesses had to build their own. Ida obtained a permit and hired contractors, and while the restaurant and an attached house were being built, she and her two children lived in a tent nearby. She opened Browder's Lunch a few days after Christmas in 1931—the first independently owned business in Boulder City. Ida was popular with the dam workers, and it was said she also ran an unofficial

Ida Browder's café under construction, December 1931.

bank at the restaurant: On payday, some of the men would give her part of their wages for safekeeping, so they wouldn't spend it in the bars in Las Vegas.

The Parent-Teacher Association met in Ida Browder's café. Ida helped organize the local Girl Scouts, a women's club, and the town's first Chamber of Commerce. After her son's death in the summer of 1932, she used his books to set up the town's first public library. But the collection was small, and she lobbied the Bureau of Reclamation for a larger library. At the end of the year a new library opened in the town administration building with a loan of three thousand books from the Library of Congress, "primarily for the school children."

For some the town was a shock. "I was into all kinds of sports in high school and all and horseback riding," said Mary Ann Merrill, who came to Boulder City from Tucson after she left high school in 1933. "I was used to things like that, and you didn't get them up here. I was quite into tennis, into the tournaments down in Tucson, and there was no tennis courts here. And the swimming—I was always into that, and there was no swimming pool....I had been in a dancing class for a good many years, and I had to give that up, you know. I mean, we came here and there was none of that."

As with the school, residents depended on the federal government for recreation and other facilities. In the spring of 1932, they asked Congress for money to build a pool. "Since the hot weather has come, the children are beginning to feel the need of a swimming pool," wrote the student editors of *Boulder Pebbles*, the town's weekly school newsletter. Congress turned down the request, so the town improvised: The fire department set up hose sprays on holidays, and on hot afternoons the movie theater opened for children so they could get out of the heat. And with so much construction material and equipment available, some could be spared: Six Companies diverted material and resources from building the dam to build a tennis court in town.

But for families leaving behind lives ruined by the Depression, Boulder City was a place to remake a life. "We found Boulder City a very friendly place," said Edna French. "Everyone was more or less on the same footing. Most people came here because they needed a job."

"It was Depression times," said Dorothy Nunley. "Everybody was in the same boat."

They shopped, went to cafés and the movies, improved their houses, and got to know their neighbors. Children played in the yards, and babies were born on cottage porches. Boulder City quickly grew into something more than a construction camp. It became a home, and a community.

"A pernicious practice which should be stopped"

Mary Ann Merrill found a job at Smith's Root Beer Stand as a carhop, bringing orders out to customers to eat and drink in their cars. She earned only a dollar per shift in wages, but in a good shift she could make another five or six in tips. "That was usually on payday," she said, "because the day after they probably wouldn't have any money left."

With thousands of men at work, payday brought a lot of cash to Boulder City. It arrived every two weeks in a convoy from Las Vegas. "They'd bring it out from Vegas under guard," said Tex Nunley. "Rangers in front of the car that had the money, and rangers behind. They brought it into the Six Companies place where they paid off. There was a dorm right across the street, and they had machine guns up there on the top floor that were set up there on the door where you went in, where they kept the money. There never was a robbery."

"It was a great time when they brought the payroll in," said Alice Hamilton. While the police guards cleaned their guns inside, boisterous workers lined up at a window at the back of the building to cash their paychecks. "The language was very coarse sometimes," said Alice.

But the cash was quickly distributed and spent. Families had to cover rent, utilities such as water and electricity, transport to work, meals, groceries, laundry, and other essentials out of wages of $4 or $5 a day. It was enough: "There's a lot of people worked here that I know in Boulder City and Las Vegas that raised a big family, and educated them on four dollars a day," said one resident, William McCullough. But not more than enough: "You could live on it in those days, but you couldn't hardly," said Erma Godbey.

A lot of the money found its way back into Six Companies' accounts. Men living in company dormitories and eating in the mess hall, or living in company cottages, had charges for rent and meals deducted from their pay. Those who had drawn scrip from the company had to pay it back. Scrip was an advance on a worker's wages: If he was short of money between paydays, he could apply at the Six Companies office for a book of coupons that could be exchanged for groceries and other goods at the Boulder City Company Store. It was like a loan—but a loan that could be spent only in one place. By issuing scrip, Six Companies guaranteed that wages would be spent at its own store.

Scrip was easily abused. There were some things that the company store didn't sell—gasoline, for example. If a worker was short of money and needed gas, he could draw scrip and sell it for cash—but often not at full value. People with money could take advantage of people without and pay, say, $4 in cash for $5 worth of scrip.

Scrip also made it hard for other businesses to compete with the Boulder City Company. When the Bureau of Reclamation began issuing permits for new businesses, it limited the number of retail stores. The bureau's goal was to stop Boulder City being overrun by people hoping to make quick money in a growing town where everyone was employed. But the effect was to restrict competition. Four out of five workers in town were employed by Six Companies, and in an emergency the availability of scrip meant they could keep shopping at the company store when they couldn't shop elsewhere. "Most all of them had emergencies," said Tex Nunley. "I know I did."

Six Companies argued that scrip provided a service to its employees and that the alternative would be to pay them every day—"an impossibility," it said. But other business owners in Boulder City—and as far away as Las Vegas—saw it as giving the Boulder City Company an unfair advantage. Others, including some politicians, saw it as Six Companies exploiting its workers. "The Six Companies pays off with coupon books between pay days," argued the Wobblies' newspaper, *Industrial Worker.* "These are good only at the company store. It keeps the money in the hands of the Six Companies. If they paid cash the men might go to Las Vegas and buy things they needed at a reasonable price." It was "a pernicious practice which should be stopped," complained Senator Tasker Oddie of Nevada. "Our government pays the contractors what is due them in cash and they should pay their employees in cash and in nothing else."

In 1933, the new administration of President Roosevelt agreed—at least on the matter of scrip. Roosevelt's secretary of the interior, Harold Ickes, told the newspapers, "I believe a man is entitled to his salary in money, not scrip," and he instructed Six Companies to stop issuing it that May. The company continued to make a profit from housing and the mess hall, but outlawing scrip limited its financial hold over its employees. It was yet another way in which life in Boulder City was becoming less like life in a construction camp and more like an everyday town.

For many families a paycheck covered living expenses and not much more. Some saved what they had left over: Hobart Blair's family of three lived on a dollar a day and saved the rest of Hobart's pay—enough in a year to buy a new Chevrolet costing $750. There was no bank in Boulder City, so Carl Merrill deposited his extra cash at the post office—"it was like putting it in the bank"—and so did others: At the end of September 1932, the Boulder City Post Office reported almost $200,000 on deposit in personal savings accounts. Some workers sent money to support family elsewhere in the country: During the previous three months, the post office issued $155,000 worth of money orders that could be mailed.

Others spent. For some workers with money in their pockets, payday meant piling into cars and driving to Las Vegas. There was no alcohol, and no bars, in Boulder City. Until the end of 1933, during the period known as Prohibition, alcohol was banned throughout the United States. But the law was openly disregarded in Las Vegas. Rowdy groups of high scalers, miners, truck drivers, and other workers gathered to drink cheap bootleg—illegal—liquor. For those who didn't want to drive all the way to Las Vegas, there were bars and casinos along the highway, starting just beyond the gatehouse. "They went out there to let off steam," said Lillian Whalen. "When men worked in such dangerous and such unpleasant surroundings as a lot of the work at the dam was, you couldn't blame a lot of the fellows for sort of letting their hair down."

"Probably every second or third building on Fremont Street...was a saloon or a gambling hall, or both," remembered Bruce Eaton. "They never closed them." Besides ignoring the prohibition of alcohol, Las Vegas also legalized gambling in 1931. Tourists came to the city to sightsee the dam by day and visit the casinos and bars by night. The tourists'

Bars and casinos on Fremont Street in Las Vegas, 1932.

money and the dam workers' wages meant that the small desert city in Nevada avoided some of the worst effects of the Great Depression.

When their pay was spent, workers hustled back to Black Canyon for the start of the next shift. Or they were rounded up: "Sometimes they'd send me in to get some of our key men, like skiptenders, engineers, even the hard-rock miners and powdermen," said Bud Bodell, the Six Companies' security chief. "I'd take a truck in, pick 'em up, and take 'em back to work. I'd find them in every saloon in town, too sick to go to work, or forgot to go to work."

"They never left anybody buried in the dam"

Arriving back on the job in the summer of 1934, the men found Hoover Dam more than half-finished and growing fast. In June, just a year after the first bucket had been emptied in the bottom of Black Canyon, the two millionth cubic yard of concrete was poured on the dam. In July, the number of men employed on the project reached its peak, at 5,251. The structure climbed up past the railroad trestle on the canyon wall and swallowed its steel legs. The gaps between the columns were filled and the dam looked more like a solid wall and less like a pile of blocks.

Engineers had calculated that if the vast mass of concrete needed to build Hoover Dam was poured in one piece, it would take 125 years to harden. Concrete cures because of a chemical reaction between cement and water, which produces heat. In a small mass, the surrounding air

Construction of Hoover Dam at its height. The two emergency spillways are nearing completion (bottom right and top left); the intake towers are rising from their foundations in the canyon walls; and in the center, the columns of the dam have reached more than half their full height. Railroad tracks snake along the canyon rim and onto an elevated trestle to deliver concrete from the Hi-Mix plant (center right), and a footbridge soars over the canyon.

carries the heat away, and the concrete hardens quickly, but in a structure the size of Hoover Dam the heat deep inside can't escape, and the concrete remains liquid. Concrete also shrinks as it cools, which can cause it to crack. That was why engineers designed the dam to be built in separate columns—to avoid ending up with a dam that was soft in the middle and cracked on the outside. The columns allowed air to circulate, and once the concrete had cooled and shrunk, the gaps between them were filled to create a strong, solid structure.

They also designed a huge cooling system to speed up the curing process. Small one-inch-diameter pipes were laid in the concrete as it was poured, spaced five feet apart—more than 660 miles of them in total, looping through the dam from an eight-foot-wide gap in the middle called the slot. From there they were connected to a cooling plant built on the lower cofferdam: "an ammonia compression system similar in most details to those used in making ice," in the words of the engineers—or in everyday words, a giant refrigerator. It was capable of chilling and pumping more than two thousand gallons of water per minute through the pipes embedded in the concrete. Thermometers measured the dam's temperature, and when the concrete had cooled and hardened, the pipes were disconnected and pumped full of cement to make the structure solid. The slot was gradually filled from the bottom. Like much in the building of Hoover Dam, this was new technology: the first time a refrigeration system had been used to cure a concrete structure of such size.

With so much concrete being poured at such speed by so many men, there were stories of workers being left buried—but they were just that: stories. "They never left anybody buried in the dam," said Bob

Parker. Leaving another worker's body behind would have been unthinkable to the men, and because the dam was built up in thin layers, there wasn't much opportunity for it to happen. When someone did get trapped, they were immediately dug out. In November 1933, a form at the top of a column collapsed, burying W. A. Jameson in an avalanche of wet

The slot, an eight-foot-wide gap in the middle of the dam where a network of cooling pipes was connected to a refrigeration plant. In this 1935 photograph, the bottom half of the slot has been filled with concrete, and the top half is still open.

concrete. Jameson's colleagues spent the next two shifts excavating his body from the debris.

But suspicions persisted that Six Companies was undercounting deaths to make its safety record look better and avoid claims for compensation. In the summer of 1933, former workers began filing lawsuits against Six Companies seeking damages for injuries and illness resulting from carbon monoxide poisoning during construction of the diversion tunnels. Hoping to cast doubt on all of them, Six Companies used its influence in Las Vegas to see that the first of these cases to reach court was the weakest. To damage the reputation of the worker who filed the lawsuit, agents working for the company recruited him to take part in a robbery and made sure he was caught. To discredit his claims that he had been permanently disabled, they took him to parties where he drank large amounts of liquor, danced, played the piano and sang, and was introduced to women who testified to having had sex with him.

Despite Six Companies' efforts the jury was unable to reach a verdict, and the lawsuit ended in a mistrial. A second carbon monoxide case, tried in February 1935, was different: The jury heard the evidence and quickly reached a verdict—in favor of Six Companies. Almost immediately, evidence surfaced that members of the jury had been bribed. Lawyers for the plaintiff protested and asked for a retrial, but the judge refused.

In both cases Six Companies had flexed its muscles and broken the law, and succeeded in avoiding payouts—but it did not succeed in stopping the lawsuits. Forty-eight more were filed, with claims for damages totaling $4.8 million. Perhaps realizing that it couldn't go on discrediting plaintiffs and bribing jurors, the company settled the cases out of

An injured man is loaded into an ambulance on the construction site.

court—but it never admitted responsibility for carbon monoxide poisoning.

Officially, 105 work-related deaths had been recorded by Memorial Day 1935, when a plaque commemorating the dead with the inscription "They Labored That Millions Might See a Brighter Day" was unveiled at the damsite. Senator Pat McCarran of Nevada spoke of "the remarkable safety record set during the project's building," and Walker Young said, "That more lives were not lost is evidence of the effort made to avoid accidents and speaks well for the caliber of the workmen themselves." Only one speaker, John Sherwood, president of the Nevada Federation of Labor, called Six Companies and the Bureau of Reclamation to account, blaming "lack of progress" by employers as "responsible for the fatal and disabling accidents which have occurred here." "Human rights,

April 1935: Walker Young (left), Frank Crowe (second from right), a Las Vegas auto dealer, and a Union Pacific representative make the first official car crossing of Hoover Dam. Behind them, the tops of the four-hundred-foot intake towers are being finished.

Sherwood believes, should be put on the same basis as property rights," explained the *Las Vegas Evening-Review*.

Meanwhile, the dam these men had died building was almost finished. The contract between Six Companies and the government had called for concrete pouring to *start* on December 4, 1934. By that date the dam was more than 90 percent complete, and almost two years ahead of schedule. Shortly afterward, it reached its full height: "'K' Block Hits 727 Foot Mark and First Part of Dam Is Finished," read the headline in the *Las Vegas Evening Review-Journal* on February 7, 1935. The intake towers behind the dam were 98 percent complete, the paper reported, and the concrete powerhouse at its foot that would house the electricity-generating turbines was three-quarters finished. "Of the 4,421,000 yards of concrete in the entire project, 4,086,000 have been poured," the paper wrote.

May 29, 1935: Frank Crowe (second from left) looks on as the final few yards of concrete are poured in the top of the slot, completing the main structure of Hoover Dam.

Two months later, Frank Crowe and Walker Young, along with a Las Vegas auto dealer and a representative of the Union Pacific Railroad, made the first official car crossing of the dam on the new highway connecting Nevada and Arizona, US 93, which ran across the top of the dam. But the concrete underneath was still cooling. It wasn't until the following month that the last refrigeration pipes in the slot were disconnected and pumped full of cement. On May 29, 1935, a mixing truck backed up to a gap in the roadway, and the last few feet of the slot were filled with concrete. The main structure of Hoover Dam was finished.

As the labor-intensive work of delivering and pouring concrete slowed down, Six Companies began laying men off. Many were unskilled, leaving behind welders, pipe fitters, electricians, and other skilled workers for the work that remained. At the beginning of 1935, just six months after employment on the project had peaked, the number of men on the company's payroll fell below three thousand, and in February Frank Crowe announced that the night—or graveyard—shift would end. It was the first time since 1931 that work was not going on around the clock.

The government had expected that people would leave Boulder City when work was finished and that the population would shrink to just a couple hundred Bureau of Reclamation employees operating the dam. Six Companies had planned to tear down the shoebox houses it had built in town. But families had made homes, and many decided to buy their houses and stay. The price for a house was $250.

Others who were laid off packed up to look for work elsewhere, and neighbors and friends moved away.

"It was kind of a sad time," said Mary Eaton.

"It was sort of like breaking up your own family," remembered Tex Nunley. Those who remained weren't certain how much longer they'd have a job.

"My husband would come home from work," said Mary, "and he'd say, 'Well, I worked today. I don't know about tomorrow.'"

The end of the Colorado River in Mexico, photographed in 2009. The Colorado has not reached the Gulf of California regularly since the 1960s. Stored and diverted by a chain of nine dams on its main section and dozens of others on its tributaries, the water in the river has been completely consumed by farms and city water utilities. Two miles south of the Morelos Dam, on the US-Mexican border, what remains collects in a shallow pool and vanishes.

FIVE

THE END OF THE RIVER

"The waters of the great stream were...quiet and gentle"

FEBRUARY 1, 1935. A FEW MINUTES AFTER THE START OF THE DAY SHIFT, Frank Crowe threw a switch, and winches began lowering a 2.5-million-pound steel gate into the entrance to diversion Tunnel 4. It descended steadily, then jammed. Trash carried by the river was stuck underneath, and the gate had to be raised again so it could be cleared. But after a little more than an hour it dropped all the way into place. Giant concrete plugs had already been cast in the other diversion tunnels, sealing them permanently; when the steel gate closed off Tunnel 4, the Colorado River was trapped behind Hoover Dam for the first time. Seven hundred feet above, crews were still pouring concrete, but the dam had begun doing the job it was built to do. "Like a mighty untamed bronco of other days, the Colorado River was corralled this morning," declared the *Las Vegas Evening Review-Journal*, "and after a short struggle broken to do the will of man for all time, after running wild thru the western ranges since the beginning of the world....Today the waters of the great stream were as quiet and gentle as though they had always been man's servant."

For now, valves in the plug in Tunnel 1 remained open so that the river could bypass the dam, allowing farmers downstream in the Imperial Valley to draw water to irrigate their crops. As the river rose in the spring and there was more water than they needed, the flow could be adjusted.

February 1, 1935: A steel gate closes the entrance to Tunnel 4, trapping the Colorado River behind Hoover Dam.

The dam would act like a faucet, allowing enough water through to meet the needs of farmers and others, and the reservoir behind it would fill. Meanwhile, the third and last phase of the construction of Hoover Dam had begun: installing the network of pipes and valves that would permanently manage the river flow, and the turbines, generators, and wiring that would turn it into electrical power.

Enormous steel water pipes, called penstocks, were made in sections at a specially built mill a mile from the damsite and moved carefully down the road to the canyon rim, where they were picked up by the biggest of the cableways, lowered to the mouths of the tunnels, and maneuvered into place on rails. The largest sections were thirty feet in diameter and weighed more than 150 tons and were transported on a specially built trailer towed by two Caterpillar tractors: one in front to pull, and the other behind to act as a brake and stop the huge load from running away on the steep, twisting road. Crowds came to watch them make the journey. "It was an outstanding event for everybody when we'd come down the hill with a pipe," said Curley Francis, who had changed jobs once more and drove one of the Caterpillars. "I don't know whether people just enjoyed seeing it go down the hill or [were] looking for something to happen someday."

There were four main penstocks. They would draw water from the reservoir through the four intake towers behind the dam, run through the canyon walls, and discharge downstream. Two were installed in the inner diversion tunnels, and two more in header tunnels excavated higher up in the canyon walls. Carrying hundreds of tons of water at speeds that reached eighty-five miles per hour, the pipework had to be

July 1934: The first thirty-foot-diameter section of steel penstock pipe being delivered to the damsite. A Caterpillar tractor in front pulls the load and another behind acts as a brake—and a line of anxious engineers and officials follow in cars.

flawless and strong. The walls of the biggest sections were 2.75 inches thick. They were welded together, and the welds were x-rayed to make sure they were solid. The pipes were then secured to massive concrete-and-steel anchors in the tunnels.

Smaller penstocks branched from the main lines to turbines in the powerhouse at the foot of the dam. As well as a faucet, Hoover Dam would also act like a battery: Water stored in the reservoir was stored energy; released into the penstocks, it spun the turbines, turning the stored energy into mechanical energy. The turbines spun generators, which turned the mechanical energy into electrical energy. Once operational, Hoover Dam could generate enough electricity to power a light in every house in the United States at the same time.

It would also generate money: The Bureau of Reclamation contracted with utility companies in cities in the Southwest to sell them the electricity, and over the next fifty years the income would repay the cost of building the dam—almost $109 million, plus more than $11 million in interest. The first four generators were installed for the Los Angeles Bureau of Power and Light; eventually there would be seventeen, providing power to Southern California and Arizona, as well as Las Vegas and Boulder City.

But before any electricity could be made, the water in the reservoir had to reach the intake towers and create enough pressure to drive the turbines, a level roughly 350 feet above the old river level. During the spring of 1935, the water rose, covering the cofferdam and diversion tunnel entrances and hiding the construction site in Black Canyon under a quietly growing lake. By the end of the flood season, in July, the new reservoir—which would be named Lake Mead, after Elwood Mead, the commissioner of the Bureau of Reclamation—held more than 4.6 million acre-feet of water and stretched back eighty miles into the distant desert. Then it stopped rising as the river's flow slowed during the dry months of late summer and winter, before rising again the following spring. It would be a year before the reservoir would be high enough for the generators to operate, and more than five years before it was full.

May 1935: Water fills Black Canyon behind Hoover Dam, rising toward the bottoms of the four intake towers.

While the lake rose, construction wound down. During the summer and fall of 1935, the last concrete was poured on the roof of the power-house; the last penstocks were welded into place; the water outlets in the canyon walls below the dam were finished; and the workforce dwindled from thousands into the hundreds—many of them cleaning and packing up machinery. Six Companies was anxious to complete its contract and get paid.

"It's one thing to build a great public works," said one of the company directors, "it's something else to get a government bureau to admit it's finished." First, the company and the government had to agree on a final price for the job. Parts of the dam's design had been changed while it was being built: Tunnels for the penstocks had been enlarged, for example, and the powerhouse was made bigger to hold additional generators. The cost of the additional work and the total amount of rock excavated, concrete poured, and other work done had to be calculated.

They also had to settle an investigation into Six Companies' payroll records. "Time Records and Payroll Checks Seized by the Government Today," reported the *Las Vegas Evening Review-Journal* on February 26, 1935. A former Six Companies employee had given the government evidence that the company had persistently broken the federal overtime law, which limited the working day to eight hours and called for a penalty of $5 to be paid to the government every time a worker exceeded the limit. The employee claimed Six Companies had violated the law more than sixty thousand times and hidden it by keeping two sets of payroll accounts. While government auditors examined the seized records, Six Companies argued furiously that the law made an exception for emergencies and that the construction of Hoover Dam in extreme conditions during the Great Depression was one long "emergency." It reminded congressmen and the public that it was finishing the dam ahead of schedule, saving the government and taxpayers money.

The dispute made no difference to the men who had worked the overtime, most of whom had already left Boulder City. Eventually, Six Companies agreed to pay a $100,000 fine. When this was settled and all the work had been accounted for and the two sides agreed the job was finished, Six Companies' final bill for building Hoover Dam was almost $55 million. After deductions for electricity and materials supplied by the government and paying the fine, Six Companies was paid $51,950,000 and made a profit estimated to be more than $10 million. It had completed the job in a little less than five years—two years, one month, and twenty-eight days ahead of schedule.

On February 29, 1936, Frank Crowe met Ralph Lowry, who had replaced Walker Young as the Bureau of Reclamation's chief engineer, on the roadway crossing Hoover Dam. A newsreel company sent a camera crew, but there wasn't a lot for them to film. "I am very happy to turn over the job for your acceptance," said Crowe. Lowry replied, "I am pleased to accept this great work and to congratulate your company upon the rapid progress made and the excellent quality of work done here." The two men shook hands, and with that, the biggest dam in the world officially became the property of the United States government.

Six Companies' work was done. The dam's work was beginning.

"You don't have to worry any more"

Five months earlier, at the end of September 1935, President Franklin Roosevelt had visited Boulder City to dedicate Hoover Dam. He toured the site and spoke to a crowd of twenty thousand who had made their way to Black Canyon, and many more on a live broadcast over the radio. After the ceremony, First Lady Eleanor Roosevelt ate lunch in the Boulder City mess hall, then returned to the canyon, where she was lowered to the powerhouse in a skip by one of the cableways. "It was a great thrill to Mrs. Roosevelt because she is a great flyer," reported the Nevada senator who visited the site with the Roosevelts. "She said it was the greatest view of the great engineering project that could not be obtained anywhere else."

"That was quite impressive, hearing him dedicate that dam," said a worker who was given the day off to hear the president's speech. "After that we went right back to work, went back to work moving that pipe again."

Roosevelt celebrated the dam's great scale, and the ingenuity and labor that had built it. "This is an engineering victory of the first order— another great achievement of American resourcefulness, skill and determination," he declared. But he spent as much time talking about what the dam would mean for the Colorado River and the western states as he did about its construction:

"The farms, the cities, and the people who live along the many thousands of miles of this river and its tributaries all depend...upon the conservation, the regulation, and the equitable division of its ever-changing water supply," the president said. "Through the cooperation of the states whose people depend upon this river, and of the federal government which is concerned in the general welfare, there is being constructed a system of distributive works and of laws and practices which will insure to the millions of people who now dwell in this basin, and the millions of others who will come here in future generations, a just, safe, and permanent system of water rights."

President Franklin Roosevelt before a crowd of twenty thousand gathered for the dam's dedication, September 30, 1935.

For people three hundred miles south in the Imperial Valley, "just, safe, and permanent" meant a steady supply of water to irrigate farmland, and an end to destructive droughts and floods. Even before the president spoke, the dam had shown them what it could do. On June 20, it caught and contained the biggest flood on the Colorado in more than three years, "for the first time removing the danger of a break in the protective system of levees that guard the Imperial Valley," reported the Bureau of Reclamation. The flood was followed by a late-summer drought. A year earlier, drought had cost Imperial Valley farms an estimated $10 million in lost crops. This year, operators at Hoover Dam released enough water from the rising reservoir behind the dam to keep the irrigation canals full and the fields wet. "What this meant to the people dependent upon the unpredictable river for their livelihood was disclosed by the joyful manner in which newspapers in the Imperial Valley told their readers, 'You don't have to worry any more,'" declared the bureau.

Then and to this day, most of the water taken from the Colorado River is used to support farming: about 80 percent, or four out of every five gallons. Only a small part goes to other industries and cities for drinking, bathing, and other uses. And because farmers in the Imperial Valley had been the first to divert water from the Colorado and put it to beneficial use, the Law of the River gave them the first claim to it, and they received a bigger share than almost any other users: nearly 60 percent of the state of California's entire allocation of Colorado River water belongs to the Imperial Valley irrigation system.

When Hoover Dam began operating, there were already nearly half a million acres of land being farmed in the Imperial Valley. Farmers there grew high-value crops for market: ten thousand acres of cantaloupes, four thousand acres of grapefruit, nearly twenty thousand acres of lettuce, and six thousand acres of peas, together with dozens of other fruits and vegetables, such as oranges, lemons, dates, grapes, tomatoes, carrots, onions, cabbage, and asparagus. They grew grains such as wheat and barley, cotton, and alfalfa to make hay for livestock. In winter, ranchers transported sheep and cattle to the valley by rail to feed.

Farmers liked to say that the fruits and vegetables grown in the Imperial Valley and raised with Colorado River water created more wealth than the Gold Rush. Today, their value is almost $2 billion a year, and two-thirds of the vegetables consumed in the United States in winter are grown there. The valley is visible from orbiting spacecraft: an otherworldly green splash across the tan desert of Southern California,

A farmworker lets water into a cantaloupe field from an irrigation ditch in the Imperial Valley, March 1937. The young cantaloupes have waxed paper covers to protect them from nighttime cold. This photograph was taken by Dorothea Lange, whose work drew attention to the lives of farmworkers in the West in the 1930s.

stretching from the Salton Sea to the US-Mexican border. Together with other parts of the southwestern desert irrigated by the Colorado, around Yuma, Arizona, and in the Palo Verde and Coachella Valleys in California, it is among the richest and most productive agricultural regions in the country. The transformation of the desert into farmland imagined a century earlier, when white settlers opened the first irrigation ditches in the Imperial Valley, had been secured by Hoover Dam.

"The Giant of Hoover Dam"

For people in the city of Los Angeles, the promise of Hoover Dam was not water, but electricity: "The first great gifts of the mighty Colorado—light and power," in the words of the *Los Angeles Times*.

Between 1920, when the first surveys for Hoover Dam were made, and 1935, when it was finished, the population of Los Angeles County more than doubled, from eight hundred thousand to over two million. On October 9, 1936, as many as half of them jammed the city's downtown for an "electrical pageant." Power-themed parade floats and marching bands made their way down Broadway; congressmen, the mayor, and other officials gave speeches in front of a giant painting of Hoover Dam outside City Hall; and street vendors offered dark glasses for sale for a dollar a pair to protect parade-goers' eyes when the electricity arrived and the lights along the route were turned on. As darkness fell, Elizabeth Scattergood, daughter of the chief engineer of the Los Angeles Bureau of Power and Light, pushed a button completing the connection between the city and the generators three hundred miles away, delivering Hoover Dam power to the city for the first time. A giant spark arced theatrically above the crowd and banks of searchlights lit up the evening sky. "Astride the power of 115,000 horses, with burning plumes outspread, the Giant of Hoover Dam—Electricity—rode into Los Angeles," wrote the *Times*.

Hoover Dam supplied half of Los Angeles's electricity in the 1940s and 1950s: electricity to power industry, such as steel and aluminum mills, shipbuilders, and aircraft manufacturers, and electricity to power lights

October 9, 1936: A pageant in downtown Los Angeles celebrates the delivery of electricity from Hoover Dam. The police estimated the crowd at one million—which if accurate would have been almost half the population of Los Angeles County at the time.

and appliances in people's homes. When the United States entered World War II in 1941, power made at Hoover Dam helped fuel the country's arms industry. Sixty-two thousand warplanes—a fifth of the military's entire wartime air force—were built in Los Angeles County. Meanwhile, the city's utility companies ran advertising campaigns for refrigerators, washing machines, radios, and other home appliances. They had signed contracts committing to buy electricity from the Bureau of Reclamation; now they had to persuade people to use it.

But the growing city also needed water, and for that it turned to the Colorado River, too. Even before Hoover Dam was finished, Six Companies began sending equipment and men—including Superintendent Frank Crowe—150 miles downriver to Parker, Arizona, where it had won a contract from the Bureau of Reclamation to build another big dam on the Colorado. If Hoover was the tallest dam in the world at the time, Parker Dam was the deepest: Almost four-fifths of it was hidden below the ground in a giant pit extending 235 feet down to reach bedrock. Only the top eighty-five feet of the structure was visible above the river.

Parker Dam stored water for Los Angeles and surrounding cities. A few miles upriver from the dam, giant pipes emerged from the new reservoir, pumping water up the rocky hillside and delivering it into the Colorado River Aqueduct: 242 miles of canals, pipes, and tunnels that snaked across the desert toward the Pacific coast. Built and paid for by Los Angeles and neighboring cities in Southern California, the aqueduct could carry one billion gallons of water a day. Gravity kept the water moving downhill, and where it ran into obstacles such as mountain ridges, siphons and pumps lifted it and sent it on its way again. The electricity to power the pumps was made at Hoover Dam.

Carrying water across the desert: Workers building the Colorado River Aqueduct, which would draw water from the Colorado River and deliver it to cities in Southern California, 250 miles away.

As California sucked water from the river—through the aqueduct for Southern Californians to drink and the All-American Canal to irrigate farmland in the Imperial Valley—neighboring states looked on with alarm. California had more people, more industry, and more farmland than they did—and as a result, more political power and more money to build the infrastructure to transport and put water to use.

Arizona, in particular, believed that California would take more than its share, and that once it started using the water it would never give it up. Although Arizona had at first joined the 1922 Colorado River Compact, it later refused to "ratify," or officially confirm, it. The compact did not determine how much water each individual state was entitled to, and Arizona wanted its share guaranteed. When the Boulder Canyon Project Act was passed in 1928, authorizing the construction of Hoover Dam, Arizona's congressmen refused to support it, believing the dam and the All-American Canal would benefit California at its expense. In 1930, Arizona sued to try to stop construction, but lost.

Construction of Parker Dam made matters worse. In the fall of 1934, as crews built a construction bridge from the California side of the Colorado River toward the Arizona side, the Arizona governor, Benjamin Baker Moeur, declared martial law in Parker and called out the Arizona National Guard to "repel an invasion" of the state. One hundred soldiers and seven officers armed with machine guns were sent "speeding across the desert and bent on halting the work," reported the *Los Angeles Times*. Earlier in the dispute, Arizona veterans had telegrammed their representative in Congress asking the navy to send the battleship *Arizona* up the Colorado. If the battleship wasn't available, they suggested a local steamboat called the *Nelliejo* could be armed and put into service instead.

Before the guardsmen or any gunboats could arrive, the secretary of the interior, Harold Ickes, calmed things down by ordering a halt

Members of the Arizona National Guard sent to Parker, Arizona, in 1934 to stop construction of Parker Dam.

to work—and then taking the state of Arizona to court. Eventually an agreement was reached, and Parker Dam was completed in 1938. A few months later, in January 1939, the Colorado River Aqueduct began operating.

But the argument between Arizona and California went on. In 1952 Arizona sued California in the US Supreme Court. The case turned into one of the longest running in the court's history, but when it finally ended, in 1963, Arizona had got what it wanted: The court ruled that the state was entitled to 2.8 million acre-feet of Colorado River water per year, more than a third of the lower basin's share. When the case was settled, work began on the Central Arizona Project: a new canal to send Colorado

River water from the Parker Dam reservoir three hundred miles east to the cities of Phoenix and Tucson.

The Supreme Court could settle arguments between the states. But it did not have the power to decide how much water there was *in* the Colorado River, and whether it would be enough for Arizona and California, and the many other claims made on it.

"The river was nowhere and everywhere"

When Hoover Dam was being planned, engineers estimated the quantity of water that flowed down the Colorado every year to be 17.5 million acre-feet. That number became the basis for the water use agreements that divided up the river: the Colorado River Compact, which allocated 7.5 million acre-feet a year each to the upper and lower basins, plus another 1 million acre-feet to the lower basin when there was a surplus available; and later the treaty that guaranteed Mexico 1.5 million acre-feet per year.

What the engineers did not recognize was that the first two decades of the twentieth century were unusually wet. During the 1930s, which were dry years, the yearly flow of the Colorado was about thirteen million acre-feet, and over the entire twentieth century the average turned out to be about fifteen million acre-feet. So even as Hoover Dam was being built and began operating, the Colorado River suffered a structural deficit—meaning that users had the legal right to take more water out of the river every year than rain and melting snow put in.

But at the time, they were not taking all the water the agreement said they were entitled to, and by storing water Hoover Dam disguised the shortage. In dry years, the reservoir could supplement the river's natural flow, and in wet years it could be replenished. But even the vast amount of water in Lake Mead—as much as flowed down the river in two years— might not be enough to cover long droughts. And Hoover Dam was in the lower Colorado River Basin. The Law of the River obligated users in the upper basin to allow 7.5 million acre-feet to pass into the lower basin every year. In dry years, there might not be enough left for them to claim all of their share.

The answer provided by the Bureau of Reclamation was another dam. In 1956, construction began on Glen Canyon Dam, in the upper basin a hundred miles north of the Grand Canyon on the border between Arizona and Utah. It was 710 feet tall—just slightly lower than Hoover Dam—and created a reservoir, Lake Powell, that could hold twenty-six million acre-feet of water—just slightly less than Lake Mead. It almost doubled the amount of Colorado River water that could be managed by the bureau.

When the dam opened in 1963 all seven US states in the Colorado River Basin had a store of water. But others also had a claim to the river. Among them were the Indigenous nations of the basin. In 1908, the Supreme Court had ruled that Indigenous reservations had water rights and that these rights were senior—that is, they had to be met before others. But the court hadn't decided how much water Indigenous nations might be entitled to or how that amount would be calculated. That changed in 1963. When the court decided the case of *Arizona v. California*, it also ruled that Indigenous nations were entitled to enough water to irrigate

Glen Canyon Dam, the last dam built on the main part of the Colorado River, after it was finished.

all the land that could be farmed on their reservation lands. That turned out to be a lot: for the Indigenous peoples of Arizona, California, and Nevada, 761,000 acre-feet of Colorado River water per year—more than two and a half times the amount allocated to the state of Nevada. The court also ruled that this amount had to be counted as part of the water allocation made to the states where the reservations were located—so if, for example, the state of Arizona wanted to use all its water allocation, it would have to reach a settlement with the Indigenous people of the state, who could claim the water first. For most of a century, since they had been forced onto reservations by the United States government, the Indigenous people of the Colorado Valley had had "paper" water: the right to it in theory, but not the resources or the power to put it to use. Now they had "wet" water: a defined quantity of a valuable natural resource that could irrigate land, provide farm produce, and generate income.

To the south, the nation of Mexico also had a claim to the Colorado River, but it was at the mercy of the United States, which had built Hoover Dam to store water and the All-American Canal to make sure it stayed north of the border on its way to the Imperial Valley. The two countries had been unable to agree on how much should be allowed to cross the border. But as the dam rose and the canal was being dug, they restarted negotiations, and in 1944 they finally agreed to a treaty guaranteeing Mexico 1.5 million acre-feet of water a year. It was a third of what Mexico wanted, but twice what people north of the border thought it deserved. The chairman of the Imperial Irrigation District complained that the United States government had failed to protect its citizens' "property rights."

With water guaranteed, Mexico built a dam on the Colorado. The Morelos Dam, finished in 1950, was not far from the place where the river had burst its banks in 1905 and the story of Hoover Dam had begun. There, the river forms the international boundary, so one end of the dam was in Mexico and one end was in the United States.

Unlike Hoover and Glen Canyon, which were storage dams, Morelos was a diversion dam: It forced the river to make a hard turn to the west, into a canal that irrigated farms in the Mexicali Valley, but it did not create a reservoir. For a time after it was completed, what remained of the Colorado River flowed on past the dam to the Gulf of California, as it always had. As it approached the gulf, it divided and wandered through three thousand square miles of wetlands teeming with fish, birds, deer, bobcats, coyotes—even jaguars. "The river was nowhere and every-where," wrote a naturalist who explored the wetlands by canoe in the 1920s. "He meandered in awesome jungles, he all but ran in circles, he dallied with lovely groves, he got lost and was glad of it."

The Morelos Dam, photographed in 1973. The Colorado River is diverted into an irrigation canal (right), allowing only a narrow stream to continue south. One end of the dam is in the United States (left), the other in Mexico (right).

But in 1963, Glen Canyon Dam began operating, and Lake Powell began to fill. The United States continued to allow 1.5 million acre-feet of water a year to cross the border into Mexico, as it had agreed—but that was all, and all of that was diverted for irrigation. Now just a trickle found its way past Morelos Dam, and none reached the ocean. A few miles to the south it collected in a shallow pool and disappeared into the dry ground. The wild river that had once torn down out of the Rocky Mountains, carved the canyons of the desert, and soaked the marshes and wetlands of the delta was gone.

"The father of all the dams"

"Can you imagine depriving five million people a year of recreation, let alone drinking water, the electric lights and all that kind of thing you get out of a project?" asked Walker Young, years after Hoover Dam was finished. The commissioner of the Bureau of Reclamation when Glen Canyon Dam was built, Floyd Dominy, once said the Colorado River without dams was "useless to anyone." The men who built dams and water management systems along the Colorado had an unshakable belief in their benefits and couldn't imagine the modern American West without them.

But even as the dams were being built, others had begun to question whether they were necessary. Glen Canyon Dam flooded one of the most beautiful wild canyons in the West. Along its length the Colorado River had carved mazes of side canyons and waterfalls, and arches and natural amphitheaters so magnificent and still that they had been given names like Music Temple, Tapestry Wall, and Cathedral in the Desert. "The

Cathedral in the Desert, a natural amphitheater sculpted by the Colorado River, photographed in the late 1950s, before Glen Canyon was flooded. Pictures like this were published by the Sierra Club and others in the environmental movement and helped familiarize people with the natural beauty of the remote desert.

canyonlands did have a heart, a living heart, and that heart was Glen Canyon and the golden, flowing Colorado River," wrote one person who saw the canyon before it was submerged.

But Glen Canyon was remote, more than thirty miles from the nearest paved road before the dam was built, and few people knew of it. Not so the Grand Canyon, which was visited by hundreds of thousands of people every year.

Even before Hoover Dam was built, the Bureau of Reclamation had proposed building dams that would partly flood and dramatically change the Grand Canyon. Bridge Canyon Dam, at the southwestern end, would be taller than Hoover Dam and create a reservoir that would flood thirteen miles of Grand Canyon National Park and forty miles of the adjacent Grand Canyon National Monument. Marble Canyon Dam, at its northeastern end, would divert most of the Colorado River around the canyon through a tunnel, leaving only a stream behind "for scenic purposes." Neither dam was intended to store water or control flooding. They were known as "cash register" dams because their purpose was to generate electricity and pay for later water management projects elsewhere—for example, powering the pumps that sucked water from the Parker Dam reservoir into the Central Arizona Project canal, hundreds of miles to the south.

The scenic stream the Bureau of Reclamation imagined leaving to pass through the Grand Canyon would be less than one seventeenth of the existing flow of the river—which was "entirely inadequate," the National Park Service said. "The remaining trickle would be sham and mockery in comparison to the once great force that carved the canyon—the Colorado River." Both dams were angrily opposed by environmentalists, led by the Sierra Club. Its leader, David Brower, had successfully fought the bureau's plans to build a dam in another national park, the Echo Park Dam, which would have flooded fossil beds in Dinosaur National Monument in Colorado. When the Bureau of Reclamation argued that the Bridge Canyon Dam reservoir would enable people to get better views of the lower Grand Canyon from boats, the Sierra Club ran advertising in

SHOULD WE ALSO FLOOD THE SISTINE CHAPEL SO TOURISTS CAN GET NEARER THE CEILING?

EARTH began four billion years ago and Man two million. The Age of Technology, on the other hand, is hardly a hundred years old, and on our time chart we have been generous to give it even the little line we have.

It seems to us hasty, therefore, during this blip of time, for Man to think of directing his fascinating new tools toward altering irrevocably the forces which made him. Nonetheless, in these few brief years among four billion, wilderness has all but disappeared. And now these:

1) There are proposals before Congress to "improve" Grand Canyon. Two dams would back up artificial lakes into 148 miles of canyon gorge. This would benefit tourists in power boats, it is argued, who would enjoy viewing the canyon wall more closely. (See headline). Submerged underneath the tourists would be part of the most revealing single page of earth's history. The lakes would be as deep as 600 feet (deeper for example, than all but a handful of New York buildings are high) but in a century, silting would have replaced the water with that much mud, wall to wall.

There is no part of the wild Colorado River, the Grand Canyon's sculptor, that would not be maimed.

Tourist recreation, as a reason for the dams, is in fact an afterthought. The Bureau of Reclamation, which has backed them, has called the dams "cash registers." It expects the dams would make money by sale of commercial power.

They will not provide anyone with water.

2) In Northern California, four lumber companies have nearly completed logging the private virgin redwood forests, an operation which to give you an idea of its size, has taken fifty years.

Where nature's tallest living things have stood silently since the age of the dinosaurs, much further cutting could make creation of a redwood national park absurd.

The companies have said tourists want only enough roadside trees for the snapping of photos. They offered to spare trees for this purpose, and not much more. The result would remind you of the places on your face you missed while you were shaving.

3) And up the Hudson, there are plans for a power complex—a plant, transmission lines, and a reservoir near and on Storm King Mountain—effectively destroying one of the last wild and high and beautiful spots near New York City.

4) A proposal to flood a region in Alaska as large as Lake Erie would eliminate at once the breeding grounds of more wildlife than conservationists have preserved in history.

5) In San Francisco, real estate interests have for years been filling a bay that made the city famous, putting tract houses over the fill; and now there's a new idea—still more fill, enough for an air cargo terminal as big as Manhattan.

There exists today a mentality which can conceive such destruction, giving commerce as ample reason. For 74 years, the Sierra Club (now with 46,000 members) has opposed that mentality. But now, when even Grand Canyon is endangered, we are at a critical moment in time.

This generation will decide if something untrammelled and free remains, as testimony we had love for those who follow.

We have been taking ads, therefore, asking people to write their Congressmen and Senators; Secretary of the Interior Stewart Udall; The President; and to send us funds to continue the battle. Thousands *have* written, but meanwhile, Grand Canyon legislation still stands a chance of passage. More letters are needed and much more money, to help fight the notion that Man no longer needs nature.*

*The previous ads, urging that readers exercise a constitutional right of petition, to save Grand Canyon, produced an unprecedented reaction by the Internal Revenue Service threatening our tax deductible status. IRS says the ads may be a "substantial" effort to "influence legislation." Undefined, these terms leave organizations like ours at the mercy of administrative whim. (The question has not been raised with any organizations that favor Grand Canyon dams.) So we cannot now promise that contributions you send us are deductible—pending results of what may be a long legal battle.

The Sierra Club, founded in 1892 by John Muir, is nonprofit, supported by people who, like Thoreau, believe "In wildness is the preservation of the world." The club's program is nationwide, includes wilderness trips, books and films—as well as such efforts as this to protect the remnant of wilderness in the Americas. There are now twenty chapters, branch offices in New York (Biltmore Hotel), Washington (Dupont Circle Building), Los Angeles (Auditorium Building), Albuquerque, Seattle, and main office in San Francisco.

AGE OF TECHNOLOGY
FIRST MAN 2 MILLION YRS AGO

FIRST ELEPHANTS 60 MILLION YRS AGO

FIRST REDWOODS 130 MILLION YRS AGO

FIRST MAMMALS 180 MILLION YRS AGO
FIRST DINOSAURS 180 MILLION YRS AGO

FIRST TREES 350 MILLION YRS AGO

FIRST REPTILES 275 MILLION YRS AGO

FIRST FISHES 400 MILLION YRS AGO

GRAND CANYON 550 MILLION YRS AGO
FIRST CORALS 575 MILLION YRS AGO

FIRST SPONGES 650 MILLION YRS AGO

BIRTH OF THE EARTH 4 BILLION YRS AGO

An advertisement run by the Sierra Club opposing plans to build dams that would flood part of the Grand Canyon referred to one of the most famous artworks—and tourist attractions—in the world, the ceiling of the Sistine Chapel in Italy.

national newspapers asking, "Should we also flood the Sistine Chapel so tourists can get nearer the ceiling?"

The Bureau of Reclamation fought back: The Sierra Club's status as a charitable organization, which meant it did not have to pay federal taxes, was suspended by the government the very next day after those advertisements ran.

But a tide was turning in America. In the first half of the twentieth century, when the Bureau of Reclamation was created and Hoover Dam was built, "conservation" meant saving the water in rivers by storing it and putting it to use—not "wasting" it by letting it run away into the ocean. This reflected the times: Saving and providing water was a matter of survival for people building farms and cities in the dry and thinly populated American West.

But dams don't just store rivers; they change them. Besides submerging parts of the landscape, reservoirs rise and fall as the water in them is used. In the desert, where the river is the only source of water, this means that trees and other vegetation—and animals that live on them— can't get established, leaving the shores lifeless. The water in a reservoir is also colder than the water in a free-flowing river, which affects fish and other aquatic life. Dams block fish migration. And without the annual cycle of powerful floods that scour and rearrange the riverbed, canyons become overgrown and the balance of life in them changes. In the second half of the twentieth century these and other effects of damming rivers came to be understood. At the same time, much of the infrastructure that provided people with water—the dams, aqueducts, and canals—had been built. People thought less about where their water came from, and they had more money and more time for leisure activities such as hiking and boating. "Conservation" came to mean saving the natural beauty and environment of rivers.

When the Grand Canyon was threatened, it was this version of conservation that won. Faced by opposition from environmentalists, the Bridge Canyon and Marble Canyon dams were eventually abandoned. Glen Canyon would turn out to be the last dam to be built by the Bureau of Reclamation on the main part of the Colorado River.

But people, agriculture, and industry still relied on the river—and their numbers grew. When Hoover Dam was built, roughly eight million people were living in the region supplied by the Colorado. By the beginning of the twenty-first century, there were almost forty million. Meanwhile, the amount of water in the river stayed the same—and is expected to become less, as the climate changes and drought has an impact on the amount of snow and rain that fills it every year.

In July 1983, after a winter of heavy snow followed by spring storms, Lake Mead reached its highest recorded level: Its surface was at an elevation of over 1,225 feet above sea level, less than four feet below the top of the dam. For the first and only time, Hoover Dam's emergency spillways were opened. Upriver, engineers built plywood-and-steel barriers in the spillways of Glen Canyon Dam to temporarily increase the capacity of Lake Powell and prevent a flood that might cascade down the river and threaten Hoover Dam. Lake Powell came within fractions of an inch of the level at which engineers feared they would lose control.

June 1983: Water pours into one of Hoover Dam's two emergency spillways as Lake Mead approaches its highest level on record, just four feet below the top of the dam.

Three decades later in June 2016, during a drought that by then had lasted for more than fifteen years, Lake Mead reached its lowest level on record: less than 1,072 feet above sea level. It was 120 feet above the minimum level needed to drive the generators and make electricity, and just 177 feet above what engineers call "dead pool," when water cannot be released from the reservoir and the river downstream dries up. On the walls of Black Canyon, a bleached white bathtub ring, caused by minerals left when the water was higher, showed how far the reservoir had fallen. Sixty-five miles away, a ghost town appeared: St. Thomas, which had been inundated when Lake Mead filled, emerged from the falling

March 2016: The bleached bathtub ring left on the walls of the canyon behind Hoover Dam as the level of Lake Mead approached a record low that summer.

reservoir. Elsewhere, docks and other facilities had to be moved to new locations to stay afloat. For the first time, farms, city water systems, and others were taking more water out of the river than rain and snow were putting in, and the structural deficit that existed in theory when Hoover Dam was built had become a reality. The river that had enthusiastically been called "man's servant" had begun to look overwhelmed.

The shortage gave another meaning to "conservation": saving water by using less of it. For cities and households that meant recycling and reusing water from drains and sewers, replacing thirsty grass lawns with native desert plants and landscaping, and encouraging people to

Ghost town: The foundation of a building in St. Thomas, which was flooded when Lake Mead filled, reemerged during the drought that began in 2000.

use more efficient, water-saving appliances, showerheads, and other plumbing fixtures. For farms in the Imperial Valley and elsewhere, it meant replacing flood irrigation, which simply allowed water to flow over the ground, with more efficient technology, such as sprinklers and tubes that drip water onto crops. To reduce the amount of wasted water, fields were leveled with lasers to make them as flat and even as tennis courts. Some fields were fallowed—taken out of production—to save water.

For the Bureau of Reclamation, it meant becoming a manager instead of a builder. The bureau had begun the twentieth century constructing

dams, reservoirs, and aqueducts to store and deliver water. It began the twenty-first looking for ways to improve them—for example, by lining sections of the All-American Canal with concrete to stop water seeping into the ground—and analyzing reservoir level and river flow data to find ways to manage water supplies more efficiently. Hoover and the other great dams in the Colorado River Basin still stood: concrete monoliths, holding back and diverting the river. But for the dam builders, an age of construction had come to an end.

The story of the western United States has many chapters: of colonization and war, farming and ranching, gold rushes and mining, railroads, cities, trade, and industry. Through all of them run the West's rivers and the story of water—the most precious natural resource in a dry land. At the heart of that story is Hoover Dam.

After the construction workers and equipment had left, Black Canyon fell quiet, other than for a faint hum from the machinery hidden inside the powerhouse and the tunnels. Where the muddy river had once tumbled through the canyon, Lake Mead was a still, clear, almost crystal blue. "And now it is so silent, except for a clang or so far below," said Nadean Voss, who stayed on in Boulder City. "It just seems so weird."

But the silent structure's impact stretched across the states of the Southwest and down the decades of the twentieth century. When Hoover Dam was built, it demonstrated how government could use its resources to provide work and relief in hard economic times—"a monument that was built by ingenuity and one that put bread on the tables and a roof over the heads of thousands of people during the depression," said Marion Allen. When it was finished, the concrete wall in Black Canyon had turned the wildest river in the country into the tamest and most managed. It had secured the transformation of hundreds of thousands of acres of desert into farmland and launched the growth of Las Vegas, and it provided power and water for the expansion of Los Angeles and other cities in the Southwest.

Hoover Dam and Lake Mead dwarfed anything else built in the nation, and the speed with which they were finished and their success managing the river opened the way for the dam building that would follow along the Colorado River. In the fifty years after Hoover Dam was completed, the Bureau of Reclamation built almost thirty more dams in the Colorado River Basin: in the north, high in mountains near the Green River's source in Wyoming; in the east in the Colorado Rockies, where water is stored and pumped over the Continental Divide to cities on the eastern side of the mountains; in the south, along the Salt and Gila Rivers to irrigate farmland in the Arizona desert. Eventually the world that Hoover Dam helped create would threaten to overtake it, but it was the first and remains the centerpiece of the system that delivers water, farm produce, and power to millions of people.

"The water's still held back by that dam, and it will always be that way," said Tommy Nelson.

Tommy was among the thousands displaced by the Great Depression who came to Nevada looking for work. He had been a trumpet player in Colorado, but like other businesses hit by the Depression, the dance halls where he played were closing down. "People couldn't afford to dance," he said. His father had found work at the dam, and in 1931 Tommy joined him. He worked on crews excavating the tunnels and the riverbed and was one of the last Six Companies employees to be laid off. After the dam was finished he stayed in Boulder City working as an electrician for the government. He carried on playing trumpet throughout, making extra money in dance bands in the bars near Boulder City, and in September 1935, he was part of the orchestra that greeted President Roosevelt when he came to dedicate the dam. "I was real proud to be part of that ceremony," Tommy said.

"That dam was a part of us," he added. Like many of those who built Hoover Dam, he would not forget the pride and accomplishment he felt at having been part of it and the legacy it left. On that day in September 1935, he listened as Roosevelt celebrated the labor and engineering that had built the dam and described the future it promised. "It was just wonderful, everything he had to say.

"And how true it had all been," Tommy said. "That baby is the father of all the dams."

A sunken boat emerges from the falling water in Lake Mead, June 2022.

AFTERWORD

CRISIS ON THE COLORADO

AFTER THE LOW OF 2016, THE WATER LEVEL IN LAKE MEAD ROSE slightly, before starting to fall again. In July 2022, it reached a new record low with its surface at an elevation of 1,040.92 feet above sea level. That summer, sunken boats and even dead bodies emerged from the shrinking reservoir, and the Bureau of Reclamation declared a Tier 2 water emergency. The declaration came when the lake's elevation fell below a threshold of 1,050 feet, and it triggered automatic cuts in water supply to the lower Colorado River Basin states and Mexico. Tier 1, and a first round of cuts, had been put in place the previous year, when the lake fell below 1,075 feet. Tier 3 occurs if the surface elevation falls to 1,025 feet. At the time of writing, Lake Mead and Lake Powell were 30 percent full.

Heavy snowfall in the winter of 2022–2023 means that there will be more water in the Colorado River in the short term, but the drought that began in 2000 continues—it is now the worst on record. Drought means less precipitation—rain and snow—to fill the river, and it has been accompanied by higher temperatures. Higher temperatures cause more water to evaporate from reservoirs and cause more precipitation to fall in the form of rain, which the ground soaks up more quickly than snow, which stores the water and melts slowly into the river in spring. Between 2000 and 2014, the average yearly flow of the Colorado River was almost 20 percent less than it was over the previous ninety-five years. Some studies estimate that a third of this decline is due to higher temperatures resulting from human-caused climate change; they predict that the river's flow will fall by another 20 percent by 2050 and by 35 percent by the end of the century.

But for those who depend on the Colorado, the crisis is immediate. "There's a real possibility of an effective dead pool" within two years, the general manager of the Central Arizona Project told the *Washington Post* in December 2022. Dead pool would mean no water passing through Hoover Dam: no water flowing through the All-American Canal to the farms in the Imperial Valley, no water in the Colorado River Aqueduct or the Central Arizona Project canal, and no water flowing to Mexico or the dozens of other water users in the lower Colorado River Basin. Twenty-five million people could be affected.

Faced with this possibility, households, cities, farms, and other water users, along with federal and state governments, are under continuing pressure to conserve water permanently. But the laws and customs that govern the way water users in the Colorado Basin share water from the river have made it hard for them to agree. The principle of prior appropriation, in particular, means that those who began using water first have little incentive to give up any of their rights. In April 2023 the federal government threatened for the first time to override the Law of the River and impose mandatory cuts in water use across the basin. The following month the states of the Lower Basin—Arizona, California, and Nevada—together with the region's Indigenous nations, announced an agreement to reduce the amount of water they consume by 13 percent through 2026, in return for payments from the federal government.

Others have acted locally. In Las Vegas, a 2021 law banned planting nonfunctional grass (on highway medians, for example, or around office buildings and along sidewalks), and since 1998 the city has offered residents cash to replace their lawns with native desert landscaping. The city has built an extensive system to capture wastewater and recycle it. "If it hits a drain in Las Vegas, we clean it," said John Entsminger, general manager of the Southern Nevada Water Authority. "You could literally leave every faucet, every shower running in every hotel room, and it won't consume any more water." Las Vegas has reduced its water consumption by 26 percent since 2002, while its population has grown by 750,000. At the same time, the city has made sure to guarantee its water supply for as long as possible, building an $800 million pipeline known as the "third straw," which reaches beneath Lake Mead like a bathtub drain and can draw the water from the reservoir even if it falls below the level at which Hoover Dam can operate.

Elsewhere, programs pay users to leave their water in Lake Mead. In 2019 the Colorado River Indian Tribes, whose land runs along the river around Parker, Arizona, agreed to fallow ten thousand acres of farmland, leaving 150,000 acre-feet of water in the reservoir that would have otherwise been used for irrigation. In southern Arizona, the Gila River Indian

Community permanently gave up forty thousand acre-feet of its water for conservation. In 2022, the US government provided funds to pay farmers not to use their water. But as the drought continues and water becomes scarcer, its value goes up, and some think the price offered by the government is below market value. "It's a start in the right direction," the owner of a fruit and vegetable farm in Yuma told public radio in October 2022. But he doubted the federal payments would be enough for the people in his circle.

Along with conservation measures and buybacks, there are other, more radical ideas for tackling the crisis. One proposes draining Lake Powell and relying on Lake Mead alone for water storage on the Colorado. Its supporters argue that maintaining two half-empty reservoirs makes little sense and that one full one could be managed more efficiently. They say emptying Lake Powell would restore the natural landscape and ecosystems of Glen Canyon and the Grand Canyon.

Abandoning Glen Canyon Dam and draining its reservoir is a dramatic—and so far, distant—answer to the crisis on the Colorado River and one that would have enormous impact on the landscape, the economy, and people's lives. But the same can be said of damming the Colorado in the first place. A century ago, in answer to different water needs, it was ingenuity, optimism, and a sense of common purpose that built Hoover Dam. Today those resources are needed once more, as a growing population faces a changing climate and a vanishing river.

—*May 2023*

TIMELINE

MAY 14, 1901
First water diverted from the Colorado River for irrigation in the Imperial Valley.

JUNE 17, 1902
President Theodore Roosevelt signs the Reclamation Act, creating the United States Reclamation Service (later the Bureau of Reclamation).

FEBRUARY 1905
Flooding Colorado breaks through man-made cut in levee; floodwaters flow into Imperial Valley, start to fill inland Salton Sea. Floods through November continue to widen break so much that entire river changes course.

FEBRUARY 1907
Break is closed; Colorado River resumes flow south to Gulf of California.

APRIL 1918
Reclamation Service begins investigating Boulder and Black Canyons for site to build high dam for water storage and flood control on the lower Colorado River.

JANUARY 1921
Exploratory drilling begins in Boulder and Black Canyons, continues for three years.

FEBRUARY 1922
In a report to Congress, the Reclamation Service recommends that the federal government construct a reservoir at or near Boulder Canyon.

APRIL 1922
Bill to fund construction of Boulder Canyon Project is introduced, but fails to come up for a vote; it fails again in 1924 and 1926.

NOVEMBER 24, 1922
Seven states agree to the Colorado River Compact, dividing the rights to water in the Colorado between the river's upper and lower basins.

FEBRUARY 1924
Bureau of Reclamation chooses site in Black Canyon for construction of dam.

NOVEMBER 1928
Herbert Hoover is elected president.

DECEMBER 21, 1928
President Calvin Coolidge signs the Boulder Canyon Project Act, authorizing and providing funds for the construction of Boulder Dam and the All-American Canal.

OCTOBER 1929
Stock market crash. The Hoover administration accelerates the Boulder Canyon Project in an effort to create jobs.

SEPTEMBER 17, 1930
Secretary of the Interior Ray Lyman Wilbur drives a silver railroad spike in Bracken, Nevada, beginning construction of the railroad to the construction site. Wilbur announces that the dam will be named for President Hoover.

DECEMBER 18, 1930
Secretary Wilbur approves plans for Boulder City, Nevada, a new town to house and support dam's construction workers.

JANUARY 10, 1931
Specifications and plans for the dam are published and construction bids invited.

MARCH 4, 1931
Construction bids opened. Six Companies Inc. of San Francisco offers the lowest bid, $48,890,995.50.

MARCH 11, 1931
Construction contract formally awarded to Six Companies. Frank Crowe arrives in Las Vegas to begin work as construction superintendent.

APRIL 1, 1931
Crews begin blasting walls of Black Canyon for railroad to the damsite.

APRIL 15, 1931
Boulder City post office opens after town's first buildings constructed.

MAY 14, 1931
Blasting begins for adits that will provide access to bore middle of diversion tunnels.

MAY 17, 1931
First deaths during construction of dam.

JUNE 25, 1931
Electrical transmission line from California to the damsite is completed and the power turned on.

JULY 7, 1931
Highway from Boulder City to Black Canyon is completed.

AUGUST 7, 1931
Workers strike in response to Six Companies' announcement of a pay cut. After strikers are evicted from the site and the government orders Six Companies to restart work, strikers vote to end strike on August 16.

SEPTEMBER 14, 1931
Railroad to rim of Black Canyon is completed.

SEPTEMBER 17, 1931
Blasting to enlarge diversion tunnels from the ends begins at downstream end of Tunnel 4.

JANUARY 31, 1932
First diversion tunnel is opened from end to end. All tunnels are open by April 2.

MARCH 16, 1932
Concrete lining of tunnels begins.

NOVEMBER 8, 1932
Franklin Roosevelt is elected president.

NOVEMBER 12, 1932
President Hoover visits damsite.

NOVEMBER 13–14, 1932
The Colorado River is successfully turned into the diversion tunnels, eleven months ahead of schedule.

JANUARY 1, 1933
Last load of fill dumped on upstream cofferdam.

MAY 8, 1933
Roosevelt's secretary of the interior, Harold Ickes, orders Six Companies to stop issuing scrip.

MAY 31, 1933
Excavation of riverbed completed.

JUNE 6, 1933
First concrete poured on main dam.

JULY 10, 1934
First thirty-foot-diameter steel pipe is delivered to tunnel.

JULY 20, 1934
Number of people employed building Hoover Dam peaks at 5,251.

DECEMBER 5, 1934
The three-millionth cubic yard of concrete is poured on the dam, making it 92 percent complete. The original schedule had called for concrete pouring to *start* on December 4, 1934.

FEBRUARY 1, 1935

A gate closes diversion Tunnel 4 on the Arizona side of the Colorado River, and the reservoir begins to fill behind dam.

FEBRUARY 6, 1935

Dam reaches its full height when Block K is topped out.

MAY 29, 1935

Last concrete is poured in the slot in the middle of the dam, making the structure complete.

SEPTEMBER 30, 1935

President Franklin Roosevelt visits and dedicates the dam.

DECEMBER 20, 1935

Last death during construction. Patrick Tierney falls to his death from one of the intake towers, fourteen years to the day after his father had drowned while working on a surveying crew—the second death associated with building the dam.

JANUARY 11, 1936

Top of dam is opened to the public.

FEBRUARY 29, 1936

Six Companies transfers operation of the dam to the United States government.

OCTOBER 9, 1936

Power generated at Hoover Dam is delivered to Los Angeles for the first time.

MAY 1937

Water in the reservoir reaches an elevation of 1,050 feet, the minimum level at which power can be continuously generated.

OCTOBER 12, 1940
First water delivered to the Imperial Valley via the completed All-American Canal.

JULY 1941
Reservoir behind dam is officially full after reaching 1,219 feet in elevation.

FEBRUARY 3, 1944
United States and Mexico sign a treaty guaranteeing Mexico water from the Colorado River.

APRIL 1947
An act of Congress permanently names the dam after President Hoover.

SEPTEMBER 1958
The Boulder City Act releases Boulder City from federal control.

MARCH 1963
Diversion tunnels at Glen Canyon Dam close and Lake Powell begins to fill.

JUNE 3, 1963
US Supreme Court decides *Arizona v. California,* setting the amounts of water that Colorado River Compact states and Indigenous nations are entitled to receive.

JULY 1983
Lake Mead records a record high elevation of 1,225.44 feet.

JUNE 2016
Lake Mead records a record low elevation of 1,071.64 feet. The level of the reservoir rises through 2020, before falling to a new record low of 1,040.92 feet in July 2022.

DAMS ON THE COLORADO RIVER

THERE ARE OVER A HUNDRED DAMS IN THE COLORADO RIVER SYSTEM, ranging from concrete walls hundreds of feet tall to small earth-and-rock dams on the river's many tributaries.

There are nine dams on the main stem of the Colorado, between the junction of the upper Colorado River and the Green River in Utah, and the US-Mexican border:

Laguna Dam (1909) diverted water for irrigation in the Imperial Valley in California and land east of the river in Arizona. It was the first dam built on the Colorado River.

Hoover Dam (1936) stores water in Lake Mead.

Parker Dam (1938) stores water in Lake Havasu and supplies the cities of the Los Angeles area via the Colorado River Aqueduct and the cities of Phoenix and Tucson via the Central Arizona Project canal.

Imperial Dam (1938) diverts water into the All-American Canal and irrigation systems in Arizona. The dam includes a desilting works that removes silt from the river before it enters the irrigation canals.

Headgate Rock Dam (1942) operated by the Bureau of Indian Affairs to divert water to irrigate farms on the Colorado River Indian Tribes Reservation.

Morelos Dam (1950) built by the government of Mexico to divert water for irrigation in the Mexicali Valley.

Davis Dam (1951) stores water in Lake Mohave to meet the United States' treaty obligation to deliver water to Mexico.

Palo Verde Dam (1957) diverts water for irrigation in the Palo Verde Valley in California.

Glen Canyon Dam (1966) stores water in Lake Powell.

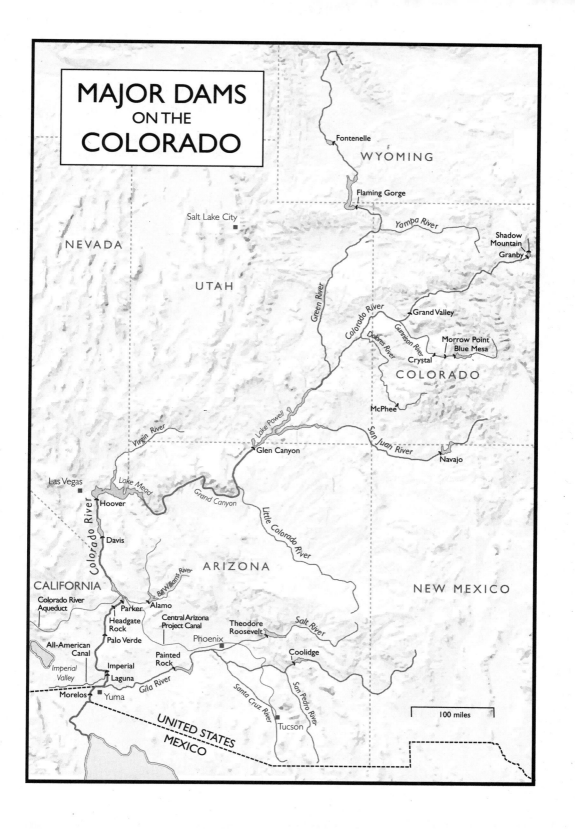

MAJOR DAMS
ON THE
COLORADO

Fontenelle

WYOMING

Flaming Gorge

Yampa River

Salt Lake City

NEVADA

UTAH

Shadow Mountain

Granby

Grand Valley

Colorado River

Dolores River

Gunnison River

Morrow Point
Blue Mesa

Crystal

COLORADO

Green River

McPhee

Virgin River

Lake Powell

San Juan River

Navajo

Glen Canyon

Las Vegas

Lake Mead

Grand Canyon

Hoover

Colorado River

Davis

Little Colorado River

ARIZONA

NEW MEXICO

Bill Williams River

CALIFORNIA

Colorado River Aqueduct

Parker

Alamo

Headgate Rock

Central Arizona Project Canal

Salt River

Palo Verde

Phoenix

Theodore Roosevelt

All-American Canal

Painted Rock

Coolidge

Imperial Valley

Imperial

Laguna

Gila River

San Pedro River

Morelos

Yuma

Santa Cruz River

Tucson

UNITED STATES

MEXICO

100 miles

Before 1921, the upper part of the Colorado River, above its junction with the Green River in Utah, was called the Grand River. The state of Colorado petitioned the US Congress to change its name because officials believed the "Colorado River" should start in Colorado and because it would strengthen the state's claim on the river's water.

Major dams on the upper Colorado and other tributaries that feed the main stem of the river:

Bill Williams River (Arizona)
Alamo Dam (1968)

Dolores River (Colorado)
McPhee Dam (1984)

Gila and Salt Rivers (Arizona)
Theodore Roosevelt Dam (1911)
Coolidge Dam (1928)
Painted Rock Dam (1959)

Green River (Utah and Wyoming)
Flaming Gorge Dam (1964)
Fontenelle Dam (1964)

Gunnison River (Colorado)
Blue Mesa Dam (1966)
Crystal Dam (1977)
Morrow Point Dam (1968)

San Juan River (New Mexico)
Navajo Dam (1963)

Upper Colorado River (Colorado)
Granby Dam (1950)
Grand Valley Dam (1917)

ACKNOWLEDGMENTS

Colleagues and friends made over a career in the publishing industry, who have taught me the craft and value of the book: authors, publishing professionals, librarians, teachers, booksellers. My thanks. You are many, and know who you are.

Those who gave assistance in the research for this work, in particular the staff at the Boulder City Library, the Boulder City/Hoover Dam Museum, and the Public Affairs Office, Bureau of Reclamation, Lower Colorado Basin Division.

The exceptional Christy Ottaviano and her colleagues at Little, Brown Books for Young Readers.

My family, always: my parents, brothers, and sons, Jonah and Alistair.

Véronique Lefèvre, for her love and friendship.

NOTES

ABBREVIATIONS:

AAUWBC: American Association of University Women Boulder City Branch Oral History Project

BCOHP: Boulder City Oral History Project

RROHP: Ralph Roske Oral History Project

UNOHP: University of Nevada Oral History Program

Introduction

2 hundreds of small earthquakes: Dean S. Carder, "Influence of Reservoir-Loading on Earthquake-Activity in the Boulder Dam Area," *Eos, Transactions of the American Geophysical Union,* October 1945, 203.

2 "A lot of these guys": Hoover Dam worker Tommy Nelson in BCOHP, Kine, Burt, and Nelson, 11–12.

2 "They hired anybody": Hoover Dam worker Jake Dieleman in RROHP, Dieleman and Dieleman, 26.

3 "He said, 'Get those trucks moving'": Tommy Nelson in BCOHP, Kine, Burt, and Nelson, 21.

3 "it wasn't any worse": BCOHP, Kine, Burt, and Nelson, 11; Dunar and McBride, *Building Hoover Dam,* 147.

4 "The miners under there": BCOHP, Allen, 6.

6 "All I could see of him": Allen, *Hoover Dam & Boulder City,* 65.

6 "I had gone quite a way...I was alright": Allen, *Hoover Dam & Boulder City,* 59–61.

6–7 "The reason I liked it...see going on": AAUWBC, Francis, 5, 11.

7 "Those trucks never turned their ignition off": Tommy Nelson in BCOHP, Kine, Burt, and Nelson, 20.

7 "could tell within an hour": AAUWBC, Francis, 6.

8 more than twenty thousand: Pettitt, *So Boulder Dam Was Built,* 110.

10 "This is a job for machines": Construction Superintendent Frank Crowe in Associated Press, "Begins 6-Year Work at the Hoover Dam," *New York Times,* March 13, 1931.

11 thirty-one million man-hours: Pettitt, *So Boulder Dam Was Built,* 114. This figure is for labor employed by Six Companies, the contractor that built the dam structure, and does not include other contractors or suppliers.

11–12 "as if our country...billions of wealth": Ray Lyman Wilbur, speech at official launch of Boulder Canyon Project, September 17, 1930, quoted in "Boulder Canyon Project Work Starts," *New Reclamation Era,* October 1930, 195.

One: The Wild Colorado
"The Colorado don't submit till it has to"

16 "I doubt as to whether": C. R. Rockwood, "Born of the Desert," *Calexico (CA) Chronicle 2nd Annual Magazine Edition,* May 1909, 25, quoted in Kennan, *Salton Sea,* 38.

17 "not serious": C. E. Grunsky in Kennan, *Salton Sea,* 46.

17 more than two billion gallons: Equivalent of the seventy-five thousand cubic feet per second in Kennan, *Salton Sea,* 58.

17 "The river chewed into Mexicali": "New River's Work," *Imperial Valley Press,* July 7, 1906.

19 some people refused to believe: Newell, "The Salton Sea," 339.

20 "The Colorado river will be sent back": "The Water's Work," *Imperial Valley Press,* July 7, 1906.

Too Thick to Drink and Too Thin to Plow

22 than almost any river in the world: Hundley, *Water and the West,* 18.

22 275 million tons: Average of annual load of suspended sediment, 1926–1930, recorded at Topock, AZ, in C. S. Howard, *Suspended Sediment in the Colorado River 1925–41,* US Geological Survey Water-Supply Paper 998 (Washington, DC: Government Printing Office, 1947), 9. Football stadium comparison is based on the volume of Texas Stadium (104,000,000 cubic feet) and a dry sand equivalent of 5,500,000,000 cubic feet to 275,000,000 tons.

23 "Ten million cascade brooks": J. W. Powell, "The Cañons of the Colorado," *Scribner's Monthly,* January 1875, 294.

24 By January 1903: Population of Imperial Valley from January 1903 to January 1905 comes from H. T. Cory, *The Imperial Valley and the Salton Sink* (San Francisco: John J. Newbegin, 1915), 1269.

27 more than $3 million: Kennan, *Salton Sea,* 90.

"The Lord left that damsite there"

27 "That Colorado River": BCOHP, Young, 11.

28 "a broad comprehensive scheme": Theodore Roosevelt, message to Congress, January 12, 1907, *Presidential Addresses and State Papers* 5: 1082–95, quoted in Hiltzik, *Colossus,* 51.

29 a million acres or more: US Reclamation Service, *Problems of the Imperial Valley and Vicinity,* 6–7.

30 "They would eat most anything": BCOHP, Young, 23.

30 "just in case": BCOHP, Young, 5.

31 "The Lord left that damsite": BCOHP, Young, 15.

"People were standing on the street selling apples"

33 as much as $130 million: Hiltzik, *Colossus,* 99.

35 More than twenty-six thousand businesses…by the end of 1930: Kennedy, *Freedom from Fear,* 58–59, 65.

35 "We should use the powers of government": Herbert Hoover, *Memoirs: The Great Depression, 1929–1941* (New York: Macmillan, 1952), 31, quoted in Kennedy, *Freedom from Fear,* 52. Although Hoover was widely blamed for the effects of the Depression and for not doing more to alleviate them, he initially advocated spending on public employment.

36 "In those days": BCOHP, Young, 17.

36 "one of man's greatest victories": "Boulder Canyon Project Construction Work Starts," *New Reclamation Era,* October 1930, 195.

36 "missed it completely": BCOHP, Garrett, 6.

"The eyes of the entire construction world"

40 "If it should fail": William L. Sibert et al., *Report of the Colorado River Board on the Boulder Canyon Project,* November 24, 1928, House Doc. 446 at 4, 70th Congress, 2nd session, quoted in Wiltshire, Gilbert, and Rogers, *Hoover Dam 75th Anniversary,* 97.

41 eighty thousand gallons: Young, "Mission of Boulder Dam Fulfilled," 353.

41 "The eyes of the entire construction world": "Eight May Bid on Dam Project," *Las Vegas Evening Review and Journal,* March 2, 1931.

41 $88,000 less..."get along without him": "Mr. Smith Would Build Hoover Dam for Less but He Omitted Check," *Denver Post,* March 5, 1931.

42 a group of companies: "Hoover Dam Bids Opened," *New Reclamation Era,* April 1931, 79. Notwithstanding its name, Six Companies was made up of seven firms: W. A. Bechtel, Henry J. Kaiser, J. F. Shea & Co., MacDonald & Kahn, Morrison-Knudsen Co., Pacific Bridge Co., and Utah Construction Co. Bechtel and Kaiser, along with a third partner, Warren Brothers, had joined the group as a single unit, thus making the six companies in the name. Warren Brothers could not come up with the cash for its share of the investment and dropped out before the bid was submitted.

Coda: Native River

45 a being called Kwikumat: Zappia, *Traders and Raiders,* 28–29.

45 Mastamho, who created the river: A. L. Kroeber, "Two Myths of the Mission Indians of California," *Journal of American Folklore* 19, no. 75 (October–December 1906): 314–16.

46 the first federally financed irrigation project: Summitt, *Contested Waters,* 151.

48 "one of the most remarkable ruins": Harry Carr, "Waters of Hoover Dam to Submerge Lost City," *Los Angeles Times,* March 13, 1932.

Two: Bosses and Men
"He had a memory like an elephant"

51 "Dam Job Head Here Wednesday": "Dam Job Head Here Wednesday," *Las Vegas Evening Review and Journal,* March 9, 1931.

51 "Crowe and his gang": Associated Press, "Mucker Boss All Set for Boulder Job," *Las Vegas Evening Review and Journal,* March 9, 1931.

52 "Any time you saw a white shirt": BCOHP, Parker, 27.

53 "That's the type he was": BCOHP, Allen, 36.

53 "walking down the road": Allen, *Hoover Dam & Boulder City,* 24.

53 "Each of the six firms": BCOHP, Garrett, 8.

54 "You can bid at your figured cost": Crowe quoted in A. E. Cahlan, "From Where I Sit," *Las Vegas Evening Review-Journal and Boulder City Journal,* February 28, 1946.

54 "He not only wanted good work": Young to Virginia Fenton, March 1, 1973, in Boulder City/Hoover Dam Museum, Boulder City, Nevada.

55 "Walker Young was a man": BCOHP, Parker, 28.

"They came with everything on their backs"

55–56 "just because they could…it was plenty hot": UNOHP, Godbey, 20–21.

56 "That was the only way we kept eating": AAUWBC, Francis, 2.

57 "They'd come with their kids: RROHP, Emery, 26.

58 "It was the most beautiful silver strand": AAUWBC, Holland, 5.

61 "The flames during the blaze": "Blaze at Dam Consumes Six Homes Today," *Las Vegas Evening Review and Journal,* March 28, 1931.

62 "and he damn near would have": RROHP, Emery, 28–29.

63 107.4 degrees…120 degrees: Wilbur and Mead, *Construction of Hoover Dam,* 35.

63 "It just seemed like it was so terrible hot": AAUWBC, Helen Holmes, 9.

63 "I told my husband": BCOHP, Godbey, 16.

63 two dormitories . . . thirty cottages: *Reclamation Era,* August 1931, 180.

64 "You were really just existing": AAUWBC, Helen Holmes, 8.

"Don't go down there"

64 there were just a few hundred…for every one person employed: *New Reclamation Era,* May 1931, 107; Kleinsorge, *Boulder Canyon Project,* 301.

64 "None should go to Las Vegas": "Warning to Unemployed," *New Reclamation Era,* March 1931, 49.

64 "already a serious problem": Associated Press, "Begins 6-Year Work at the Hoover Dam," *New York Times,* March 13, 1931.

64–65 "pitiful…anything yesterday": "A Pitiful and Pathetic Sight," *Las Vegas Age,* February 10, 1931.

65 "When we was on the way": AAUWBC, Neil Holmes, 2.

65 "Everybody would line up": Jake Dieleman in RROHP, Dieleman and Dieleman, 25.

65 "You just went out on the job": Gieck in Dunar and McBride, *Building Hoover Dam,* 27.

69 "I couldn't believe": *Mover of Men and Mountains: The Autobiography of R. G. LeTourneau* (Chicago: Moody, 1967), 174.

71 "His average age is thirty-three": *Fortune,* September 1933, 75.

71 "People well-off": BCOHP, Garrett, 5.

"That siren—oh, it scared you"

72 "Eleven Escape Death…severed from his head": "Dam Workers Injured in Blast," *Las Vegas Age,* May 9, 1931.

72 "beyond recognition": "Two Men Die in Rock Slide," *Las Vegas Age,* May 19, 1931.

73 "Narrowly escaping": "Boulder Dam Worker Is Injured," *Las Vegas Age,* June 3, 1931.

73 "Two Men Killed": "Two Men Killed, 3 Hurt in Dam Tunnel," *Las Vegas Age,* June 21, 1931.

73 "A. B. Oliver was severely burned": "Dam Workers in Hospital," *Las Vegas Age*, July 19, 1931.

73 "That siren": AAUWBC, Helen Holmes, 10.

73 Twenty-six men died…from heatstroke: "26 Deaths at Boulder Are Reported," *Las Vegas Age,* August 5, 1931; Rocha, "IWW and Boulder Canyon Project," 7–8.

74 "We dashed out there": BCOHP, Parker, 8.

74 "many, many of them": AAUWBC, Neil Holmes, 20.

74 as high as 112 degrees: Clare Woodbury, Las Vegas doctor, in Dunar and McBride, *Building Hoover Dam,* 44.

74 "There was a swelling": "Second Victim of Heat Dies Here Last Eve," *Las Vegas Evening Review-Journal,* June 29, 1931.

74 swept away and drowned: "Dam Workers Thought Dead," July 7, 1931, and "26 Deaths at Boulder Are Reported," August 5, 1931, *Las Vegas Age.*

75 "It doesn't take much to start fires": Pettitt, *So Boulder Dam Was Built,* 96.

75 "If I hadn't been a young fellow": BCOHP, Parker, 5.

"They will work under our conditions, or they will not work at all"

76 "Boulder Dam, with all its hardships": Wilson, "Hoover Dam," 369.

76 "They were going to cut": BCOHP, Godbey, 25.

78 "largely the result": "Boulder Workers on Strike," *Las Vegas Age,* August 8, 1931.

78 "to see that they didn't come back": Bud Bodell, Las Vegas sheriff's deputy, in Dunar and McBride, *Building Hoover Dam,* 49.

78 "We're not wobblies": "$5 Minimum Is Wage Demanded by Committee," *Las Vegas Evening Review-Journal,* August 8, 1931.

78 "They needed the troublemakers": BCOHP, Chubbs, 11.

78 "they will work": "Strike Brings Shutdown at Boulder Dam," *San Francisco Examiner,* August 9, 1931.

79 "As American citizens": Wilson, "Hoover Dam," 373.

79 "pale-looking…we'll—make you": Wilson, "Hoover Dam," 376–77.

79 "A man with a wife": Wilson, "Hoover Dam," 376.

80 "There was no discrimination": "Twelve Hundred Seek Dam Work," *Las Vegas Evening Review-Journal,* August 17, 1931.

Coda: All-American River

81 "to preserve American rights": Hoover, remarks at Boulder City, November 12, 1932, in *Las Vegas Age,* November 15, 1932.

82 believed that the country was entitled: This was the Harmon Doctrine. In 1895 during a dispute with Mexico over the use of water from the Rio Grande, US Attorney General Judson Harmon ruled that the United States had no obligation under international law to share water contained within its borders. See Summitt, *Contested Waters,* 183.

82 "I shall oppose": *Protection and Development of Lower Colorado River Basin: Hearings before the House Committee on Irrigation of Arid Lands on H.R. 11449,* 67th Cong. 19 (June 15, 1922), quoted in Hundley, *Water and the West,* 177.

84 Neptune, arriving…dancing in the streets: "Canal Power Expected in Six Weeks," *Imperial Valley Press,* October 13, 1940.

Three: Turning the River

"He would fire a man for even looking like he was going to slow down"

87 "Then I really did wonder": Allen, *Hoover Dam & Boulder City,* 47. Allen's father was already employed at the dam, and Frank Crowe was a family friend.

87–88 "I had never seen so many": Allen, *Hoover Dam & Boulder City,* 47–49.

88 "a man so tough"…"I'd be trampled": Allen, *Hoover Dam & Boulder City,* 49.

91 "Neither the sizzling summer heat": C. H. Vivian, "Construction of the Hoover Dam: How the Contractors Handled the Huge and Costly Program of Preliminary Work," in *Compressed Air Magazine, The Story of the Hoover Dam,* 31. Between 1931 and 1935, the trade publication *Compressed Air Magazine* printed a series of articles covering in detail the technical and other aspects of the dam's design and construction. Several were written by Six Companies or Bureau of Reclamation employees. The articles have since been reprinted in the book *The Story of the Hoover Dam.*

92 "No one working for Six Companies": BCOHP, Hall, 8.

92 "monstrosity about three stories high": Allen, *Hoover Dam & Boulder City,* 49.

93 "We could feel the vibration": Allen, *Hoover Dam & Boulder City,* 49.

93 "going pretty fast": Allen, *Hoover Dam & Boulder City,* 51.

93 "After watching it": Allen, *Hoover Dam & Boulder City,* 49.

94 "I was half way to Boulder City": Allen, *Hoover Dam & Boulder City,* 52.

"It took a little while to fill up those empty bellies"

94 "When your shift was up": Wixson in Dunar and McBride, *Building Hoover Dam*, 183.

94 "He knew if he missed": Allen, *Hoover Dam & Boulder City*, 123.

96 "You could eat as long as you could eat": BCOHP, Parker, 11.

96 "That was very interesting": Nelson in BCOHP, Kine, Burt, and Nelson, 43.

97 "We must have a place to eat": Vivian, "Preliminary Work," in *Compressed Air Magazine, The Story of the Hoover Dam*, 33.

97 "Something new": Waters, *The Colorado*, 345.

98 "The Boulder Canyon Project": Louis C. Cramton, "Business Permits at Boulder City," *New Reclamation Era*, June 1931, 118.

98 "In a sense, the Hoover Dam": Vivian, "Preliminary Work," in *Compressed Air Magazine, The Story of the Hoover Dam*, 34.

98–99 "I think one of the reasons": Allen, *Hoover Dam & Boulder City*, 103.

"You had to be dead, absolutely dead"

99 "You had to beat the other crew": BCOHP, Allen, 11.

99 "Records Are Smashed": "Week Unusually Active at Boulder as Work at River and City Reaches High Speed; Records Are Smashed," *Las Vegas Age*, January 27, 1932; Boulder Canyon Project Notes, *New Reclamation Era*, March 1932, 56.

100 "On the first shift": Allen, *Hoover Dam & Boulder City*, 59.

101 "Tests showed": Norman Gallison, "Construction of the Hoover Dam: Details of the Driving of the Four Huge Tunnels Which Will Divert the Colorado River Around the Damsite," in *Compressed Air Magazine, The Story of The Hoover Dam*, 53. Gallison was Six Companies' public relations officer.

101 "maintained a cool, clean": Gallison, "Driving of the Four Huge Tunnels," in *Compressed Air Magazine, The Story of The Hoover Dam*, 53.

101 "Driving trucks through these tunnels": AAUWBC, Francis, 8.

102 "You look down that tunnel": Gieck in Dunar and McBride, *Building Hoover Dam*, 98.

103 "They never had that": Kine in BCOHP, Kine, Parker, Godbey and Garrett, 31–32.

103 Between September 1931...during the same period: Hiltzik, *Colossus*, 285–86.

103 "If you said they died": BCOHP, Eaton, 38.

103 "You had to be dead": Tex Nunley in BCOHP, Nunley and Nunley, 11.

"By dawn the riverbed was dry"

106 "When we came home": Nelson in Dunar and McBride, *Building Hoover Dam*, 199.

106 "The ones you felt sorry for": Carl Merrill in BCOHP, Merrill and Merrill, 17.

106 more than four to one: "Clark County Returns," *Las Vegas Age*, November 9, 1932.

106 "People were pretty bitter": RROHP, McCullough, 20.

107 "Diversion of Colorado Starts Today": "Diversion of Colorado Starts Today," *Las Vegas Age*, November 13, 1932.

109 "They were really excited...the riverbed was dry": BCOHP, Chubbs, 17.

"Everything had to be clean as one could imagine"

111 "Year's End Sees Vast Amount": "Year's End Sees Vast Amount of Work on Project Finished," *Las Vegas Age*, December 24, 1932.

113 "Down below grunted": Waters, *The Colorado*, 347.

113 "We want the world to know": Mead to E. C. Schmidt, Union Pacific public relations officer, May 6, 1931, quoted in Vilander, *Hoover Dam: Photos*, 18.

116 "We dropped ourselves over": Kine in BCOHP, Kine, Burt, and Nelson, 10.

116 was reported to have saved the life: Boulder Canyon Project Notes, *Reclamation Era*, January 1933, 12.

116 "It couldn't possibly have happened": Kine in AAUWBC, Kine et al., 5.

116–18 "It was slow work...concrete pouring": AAUWBC, Francis, 9.

Coda: White Workers Only

118 understood to mean "white": For example, when Representative Phil Swing of California said he would introduce an amendment to the Boulder Canyon Project Act requiring the hiring of "American labor only," the *Las Vegas Evening Review-Journal* ran the Associated Press story on his comments under the headline "White Labor for Dam Work Urged by Phil Swing," November 28, 1930.

118 "The government felt": Duncan Aikman, "A Wild West Town That Is Born Tame," *New York Times Magazine*, July 26, 1931, 6.

119 "Some prophesied": C. H. Vivian, "Construction of the Hoover Dam: Within a Year's Time the Government Has Reared a Modern City in the Desert at a Cost of $1,600,000," in *Compressed Air Magazine, The Story of the Hoover Dam*, 39.

119 no Black men: John C. Page, acting construction engineer, to Elwood Mead, commissioner of Bureau of Reclamation, July 27, 1931, quoted in Vilander, *Hoover Dam: Photos*, 100.

120 "never heard of any refusal"..."When additions to the force": "Negroes Will Get Jobs on Project," *Las Vegas Age*, June 18, 1932.

122 ten Black men...about sixty-five: Fitzgerald, "Blacks and the Boulder Dam Project," 259.

122 "Six trained Apache": "Trained Apache High Scalers to Work on Project," *Las Vegas Evening Review-Journal,* September 1, 1932.

122 "There wasn't any colored people": Parker in UNOHP, Allen et al., 15.

122 "The representatives of the Six Companies": Page to Mead, quoted in Vilander, *Hoover Dam: Photos,* 100.

Four: A Home in the Desert
"A gigantic but workaday job"

125 "Swinging far out": "Dramatic Scene Marks Pouring Dam Concrete," *Las Vegas Age,* June 7, 1933.

126 "Just a gigantic but workaday job": "Colorado River Is Diverted," *Las Vegas Evening Review-Journal,* November 14, 1932.

127 nearly seven hundred buckets a day: The main dam required approximately 3.4 million cubic yards of concrete and was built in 624 days, an average of 5,449 cubic yards, or 681 eight-cubic-yard buckets, per day.

128 "The rumble of a great fleet": "Dramatic Scene," *Las Vegas Age.*

129 Five construction cableways: In addition to the five twenty-ton cableways above the main dam, there were several smaller cableways. A bigger government cableway was built by the Bureau of Reclamation above the powerhouse to carry loads up to 150 tons. It's still in place today. Wesley R. Nelson, "Construction of the Hoover Dam: Description of the Aerial Cableways for the Transportation of Men, Materials, and Machinery," in *Compressed Air Magazine, The Story of the Hoover Dam,* 92–97.

131 "as the dam started to grow"…"mass confusion": AAUWBC, Francis, 11–13.

132 "more wrecks than we did": BCPL Francis (1975), 11–13.

134 over six thousand: *Las Vegas Evening Review-Journal,* September 30, 1935, 3.

134 "apparently feeling": Garrett in AAUWBC, Kine et al., 15.

"That was the start of the little schoolhouse out in the desert"

135 "Of course, with the building": AAUWBC, Whalen, 11–12.

135 like shoeboxes: AAUWBC, Lawson, 2.

135 "You think you can put a house up": Cooper in Dunar and McBride, *Building Hoover Dam,* 67.

136 "they didn't dare": AAUWBC, Holmes, 17.

137 "always a big line": AAUWBC, Lawson 4.

137 "I jumped out of bed": AAUWBC, Lawson, 3.

138 An ad for the city's businesses: "Boulder City Business and Professional Directory," advertisement, *Las Vegas Age*, June 26, 1932, 2.

138 "Accountants Beat Engineers": "Accountants Beat Engineers," *Boulder City Journal*, May 20, 1932.

139 "We were trying to get away from it": UNOHP, Godbey, 30.

139 "delivered many of them": AAUWBC, Whalen, 6.

140 200 babies…340 in 1933: Pettitt, *So Boulder Dam Was Built*, 35–36.

140 the highest birth rate: Sims Ely, "Educational Facilities in Boulder City," *Reclamation Era*, November 1932, 188.

140 "One day here came": AAUWBC, Holland, 7; "To Open New School at 'Y,'" *Las Vegas Age*, January 20, 1932.

140 "they got ahold": Holland in Dunar and McBride, *Building Hoover Dam*, 126.

141 "The many new families": "Parents Talk Over School Problem," *Las Vegas Age*, December 23, 1931.

141 "outstanding ability": Ely, "Educational Facilities," 188.

142 "while two special police officers": "530 Children Start School," *Las Vegas Age*, September 27, 1932.

"We came here and there was none of that"

143 "I had been a home ec teacher": AAUWBC, French, 3.

143 first woman employed…"resigned her position": "She Got First Money Order in B.C. Postoffice," *Boulder City Journal*, April 8, 1932; "Lucille Finney to Be June Bride," *Boulder City Journal*, May 18, 1932.

144 "Only three in our class": A. D. Hopkins, "Florence Lee Jones: Story of Her Life," *Las Vegas Review-Journal*, February 7, 1999.

144 "knew all the foremen": John Cahlan, editor of the *Las Vegas Evening Review-Journal*, in Dunar and McBride, *Building Hoover Dam*, 187. Cahlan and Jones were married in 1940.

145 "Women Also Play Part": "Women Also Play Part in Building Huge Hoover Dam," *Las Vegas Age*, August 11, 1932.

145 "I would always be bottom": BCOHP, Hamilton, 3.

145 "There weren't very many jobs": Dorothy Nunley in BCOHP, Nunley and Nunley, 33; also in Dunar and McBride, *Building Hoover Dam*, 194.

147 "primarily for the school children": Boulder Canyon Project Notes, *Reclamation Era,* March 1933, 37.

147 "I was into all kinds of sports": UNOHP, Merrill, 7–8.

147 "Since the hot weather has come": Editorial, *Boulder Pebbles* school weekly in *Boulder City Journal,* April 21, 1932.

148 "We found Boulder City": AAUWBC, French, 5.

148 "It was Depression times": Dorothy Nunley in BCOHP, Nunley and Nunley, 64.

"A pernicious practice which should be stopped"

148 "That was usually on payday": Merrill in Dunar and McBride, *Building Hoover Dam,* 195.

149 "They'd bring it out from Vegas": Tex Nunley in BCOHP, Nunley and Nunley, 21–22.

149 "It was a great time…very coarse sometimes": BCOHP, Hamilton, 8, 13.

149 "There's a lot of people": RROHP, McCullough, 16.

149 "You could live on it": BCOHP, Godbey, 25.

150 "Most all of them": Tex Nunley in BCOHP, Nunley and Nunley, 22.

150 "an impossibility": Six Companies president Warren Bechtel in "Senators Hear Dam Complaints," *Las Vegas Evening Review-Journal,* August 29, 1932.

150 "The Six Companies pays off": "Sweltering and Dying at Boulder Dam," *Industrial Worker,* July 18, 1931, 1.

151 "a pernicious practice": "Senators Hear Dam Complaints," *Las Vegas Evening Review-Journal,* August 29, 1932.

151 "Our government pays": "Senatorial Quiz on Dam Looming," *Las Vegas Evening Review-Journal,* August 19, 1932.

151 "I believe a man": United Press, "Ickes Orders Abandonment of Big Six Scrip," *Las Vegas Evening Review-Journal,* May 8, 1933.

151 "it was like putting it in the bank": Carl Merrill in BCOHP, Merrill and Merrill, 14.

151 almost $200,000…$155,000 worth: Boulder Canyon Project Notes, *Reclamation Era,* December 1932, 197.

152 "They went out there": AAUWBC, Whalen, 17.

152 "Probably every second or third": Eaton in Dunar and McBride, 216–17.

153 "Sometimes they'd send me": Bodell in Dunar and McBride, 221.

"They never left anybody buried in the dam"

153 at 5,251: Annual Project History, Boulder Canyon Project, vol. 4, 14, quoted in Stevens, *Hoover Dam,* 227.

155 "an ammonia compression system": Lawrence P. Sowles, "Construction of the Hoover Dam: How the Concrete Is Being Cooled as It Is Poured," in *Compressed Air Magazine, The Story of the Hoover Dam,* 107.

155 "They never left anybody": BCOHP, Parker, 20.

156–57 a form at the top of a column…from the debris: "Jameson Body Is Found Yesterday," *Las Vegas Evening Review-Journal,* November 9, 1933.

157 former workers began filing…settled the cases out of court: Stevens, *Hoover Dam,* 206–14.

157 they took him to parties: "Attractive Spanish Senoritas Cop Spotlight in Kraus Trial Today," *Las Vegas Evening Review-Journal,* November 13, 1933.

157 Forty-eight more…$4.8 million: "6 Companies Suits Total 4½ Million," *Las Vegas Evening Review-Journal,* August 6, 1935.

158 "They Labored That Millions": "Elaborate Rites Unveil Dam Plaque," *Las Vegas Evening Review-Journal,* May 30, 1935. The plaque was replaced in 1937 with a sculpted memorial with the inscription "They Died to Make the Desert Bloom."

158 "the remarkable safety record": "Elaborate Rites," *Las Vegas Evening Review-Journal.*

158 "That more lives were not lost": "Elaborate Rites," *Las Vegas Evening Review-Journal.*

158 "lack of progress…same basis as property rights": "Elaborate Rites," *Las Vegas Evening Review-Journal.*

158 "'K' Block…have been poured": "'K' Block Hits 727 Foot Mark and First Part of Dam Is Finished," *Las Vegas Evening Review-Journal,* February 7, 1935.

160 "It was kind of a sad time": BCOHP, Eaton, 39.

161 "It was sort of like breaking up": Tex Nunley in BCOHP, Nunley and Nunley, 61.

161 "I don't know about tomorrow": BCOHP, Eaton, 39.

Five: The End of the River
"The waters of the great stream were…quiet and gentle"

163 "Like a mighty untamed bronco": "Mighty Colorado Tamed Today," *Las Vegas Evening Review-Journal,* February 1, 1935.

165 "It was an outstanding event": AAUWBC, Francis, 15.

167 enough electricity…$11 million in interest: Wesley R. Nelson, "Construction of the Boulder Dam: How the $35,000,000 Power Plant Will Appear When Fully Equipped," in *Compressed Air Magazine, The Story of the Hoover Dam,* 138.

167 4.6 million acre-feet…eighty miles: "Boulder Lake, Now 82 Miles Long, Will Take Between 3 and 5 Years to Fill," *Las Vegas Evening Review-Journal,* September 30, 1935.

169 "It's one thing to build": Felix Kahn in "The Earth Movers I," *Fortune*, August 1943, 214.

169 "Time Records and Payroll Checks": "8 Hour Violation Is Charged Dam Builders," *Las Vegas Evening Review-Journal*, February 26, 1935.

170 almost $55 million…more than $10 million: "Six Companies' Boulder Dam Contract Completed," *Reclamation Era*, March 1936, 69; Stevens, *Hoover Dam*, 252.

170 "I am very happy…work done here": "Boulder Dam Turned Over to U.S. Today," *Las Vegas Evening Review-Journal*, February 29, 1936.

"You don't have to worry any more"

171 "It was a great thrill": Key Pittman, "President Greatly Enjoyed Day Here—Pittman," *Las Vegas Evening Review-Journal*, October 1, 1935.

171 "That was quite impressive": BCOHP, Pulsipher, 37.

171 "This is an engineering victory…system of water rights": Frederick A. Storm, "President Dedicates Dam," *Imperial Valley Press*, September 30, 1935.

172–73 "for the first time"…"worry any more": "Boulder Dam Does Its Work," *Reclamation Era*, August 1935, 158, 160.

173 about 80 percent: Molly A. Maupin, Tamara Ivahnenko, and Breton Bruce, *Estimates of Water Use and Trends in the Colorado River Basin, Southwestern United States, 1985–2010*, Scientific Investigations Report 2018–5049 (Reston, VA: US Geological Survey, 2018), pubs.usgs.gov/sir/2018/5049/sir20185049.pdf.

173 nearly 60 percent: The Imperial Irrigation District has rights to 2.6 million acre-feet of California's total allocation of 4.4 million acre-feet. In times of shortage, these rights must be satisfied before those of other users. Imperial Irrigation District. See "IID History," Imperial Irrigation District, www.iid.com/about-iid/mission-vision-statements/iid-history.

173 ten thousand acres of cantaloupes…by rail to feed: Stene, *All-American Canal System*, 31.

173 $2 billion a year: It was $1.92 billion in 2015. "Water Conservation," Imperial Irrigation District, www.iid.com/water/water-conservation.

173 two-thirds of the vegetables consumed: *A Century of Service: Imperial Irrigation District* (Virginia Beach, VA: Donning, 2011), 85, www.iid.com/home/showpublisheddocument/4900/635648001335730000.

"The Giant of Hoover Dam"

175 "the first great gifts": Thomas Treanor, "Million Give Wild Ovation as Hoover Dam Lights City," *Los Angeles Times,* October 10, 1936.

175 eight hundred thousand to over two million: United States Census Bureau.

175 as many as half: The Los Angeles Police Department estimated the crowd to number one million. "Police Unable to Hold Parade Crowd in Check," *Los Angeles Times,* October 10, 1936.

175 "Astride the power": Treanor, "Million Give Wild Ovation." "115,000 horses" referred to the rating of the generators at Hoover Dam at 115,000 horsepower.

175 half of Los Angeles's electricity…and other home appliances: Louis Shagun, "50-Year-Old Hoover Dam Fulfills a Massive Promise," *Los Angeles Times,* September 22, 1985.

177 one billion gallons: "Parker Dam," Lower Colorado Dams Office, Bureau of Reclamation, July 15, 2018, www.usbr.gov/lc/hooverdam/parkerdam.html.

179 "repel an invasion": Chester G. Hanson, "Parker Dam Troops Will Leave Today," *Los Angeles Times*, November 15, 1934.

179 "speeding across the desert": Chester G. Hanson, "Parker Dam Work Stopped by Ickes; Troops May Leave," *Los Angeles Times,* November 14, 1934.

179 Arizona veterans had telegrammed: Associated Press, "Arizona Sea Dogs Demand Battleship for Dam 'War,'" *Los Angeles Times,* March 10, 1934.

"The river was nowhere and everywhere"

181 thirteen million acre-feet…fifteen million acre-feet: "Colorado River Basin Natural Flow and Salt Data," Bureau of Reclamation, November 15, 2022, www.usbr.gov/lc/region/g4000/NaturalFlow/provisional.html.

183 761,000 acre-feet…two and a half times: Summitt, *Contested Waters,* 156. Nevada's Colorado River allocation is three hundred thousand acre-feet. As of 2021, Indigenous nations have rights to 2.5 million acre-feet of water from the Colorado and its tributaries, Bureau of Reclamation, *Colorado River Basin: SECURE Water Act Section 9503(c),* Report to Congress, March 2021, www.usbr.gov/climate/secure/docs/2021secure/basinreports/ColoradoBasin.pdf.

184 "property rights": Chairman Evan T. Hewes in "Water Pact with Mexico Stirs Sharp Protests," *Imperial Valley Press,* February 7, 1944.

185 "The river was nowhere": Aldo Leopold, "The Green Lagoons," in *A Sand County Almanac and Sketches Here and There* (New York: Oxford University Press, 1949), 142.

"The father of all the dams"

186 "Can you imagine": BCOHP, Young, 46.

186 "useless to anyone": Reisner, *Cadillac Desert,* 242.

187 "The canyonlands": Edward Abbey, "The Damnation of a Canyon," in *Beyond the Wall: Essays from the Outside* (New York: Holt, Reinhart, and Winston, 1984), 95.

188 "for scenic purposes": US National Park Service, *Survey of Recreational Resources,* 133.

188 "entirely inadequate"..."the Colorado River": US National Park Service, *Survey of Recreational Resources,* 138, 142.

191–92 over 1,225 feet...less than 1,072 feet: "Lake Mead at Hoover Dam, End of Month Elevation," Bureau of Reclamation, February 3, 2023, www.usbr.gov/lc/region/g4000 /hourly/mead-elv.html.

192 engineers built...within fractions of an inch: Philip L. Fradkin, "The Year the Dam (Almost) Broke," *Los Angeles Times Magazine,* October 29, 1995, 19.

192 120 feet...dead pool: "Storage Capacity of Lake Mead," National Park Service, December 23, 2022, www.nps.gov/lake/learn/nature/storage-capacity-of-lake-mead.htm.

195 "And now it is so silent": AAUWBC, Voss, 5.

195 "monument that was built": Allen, *Hoover Dam & Boulder City,* 24.

196–97 "The water's still held back"..."father of all the dams": Nelson in BCOHP, Kine, Burt, and Nelson, 2, 56–57, 66.

Afterword

199 30 percent: *Lower Colorado Water Supply Report,* Bureau of Reclamation, May 22, 2023, www.usbr.gov/lc/region/g4000/weekly.pdf.

200 average yearly flow...by the end of the century: Bradley Udall and Jonathan Overpeck, "The Twenty-First Century Colorado River Hot Drought and Implications for the Future," *Water Resources Research* 53, no. 3 (March 2017): 2404–18.

200 "There's a real possibility": Joshua Partlow, "Disaster Scenarios Raise the Stakes for Colorado River Negotiations," *Washington Post,* December 17, 2022.

200 "If it hits a drain": Ben Tracy, "Las Vegas Becomes Unlikely Model for Water Conservation," CBS News, June 1, 2022, www.cbsnews.com/news/las-vegas-water -conservation-grass.

201 "It's a start in the right direction": Alex Hager, "Feds Will Put a Price Tag on Colorado River Basin Water to Spur Farmers to Conserve," KUNC Public Radio, KUER 90.1, October 12, 2022, www.kuer.org/health-science-environment/2022-10-12/feds-will -put-a-price-tag-on-colorado-river-basin-water-to-spur-farmers-to-conserve.

SOURCES

ORAL HISTORIES

American Association of University Women Boulder City Branch Oral History Project. Transcripts. Boulder City Library, Boulder City, Nevada.

Francis, Richard L. "Curley." Interview by Connie Degernes, March 4, 1975.

French, Edna E. Interview by Helen Littleton, November 18, 1974.

Holland, Velma. Interview by Beatrice L. Scheid, April 6, 1976.

Holmes, Helen H. Interview by Marilyn Swanson, February 12, 1975.

Holmes, Neil H. Interview by Laura Bell, February 12, 1975.

Kine, Joe, Thomas R. "Bob" Parker, Erma Godbey, and Elton Garrett. "31ers Club Remarks and Discussion." September 1973.

Kine, Mildred E. Interview by Blanche Uehling, April 7, 1975.

Lawson, Rose E. Interview by Connie Degernes and Helen Littleton, July 26, 1974.

Voss, Nadean Holcomb Laughery. Interview by Laura Bell, March 3, 1975.

Voss, Wilfred T. "Bill." Interview by Ann Chetelat, March 2, 1975.

Whalen, Lillian. Interview by Laura Bell, September 21 and November 21, 1974.

Boulder City Oral History Project. Transcripts. Boulder City Library, Boulder City, Nevada.

Allen, Marion. Interview by Dennis McBride, April 14, 1986.

Chubbs, Steve. Interview by Andrew J. Dunar, August 14, 1985.

Dunbar, Leo. Interview by Dennis McBride, June 16, 1986.

Eaton, Mary. Interview by Dennis McBride, November 15, 1986.

Edwards, Elbert. Interview by Dennis McBride, November 12, 1986.

Francis, Richard L. "Curley." Interview by Andrew J. Dunar with Teddy Fenton, August 14, 1985.

Garrett, Elton. Interview by Dennis McBride, November 10–11, 1986.

Godbey, Erma O. Interview by Dennis McBride, November 7–8, 1986.

Hall, Harry. Interview by Dennis McBride, June 20, 1986.

Hamilton, Alice. Interview by Dennis McBride, December 20, 1986.

Kine, Joe, Leroy Burt, and Tommy Nelson. Interview by Dennis McBride, July 3, 1986.

Merrill, Carl, and Mary Ann Merrill. Interview by Dennis McBride, June 24, 1986.

Nunley, Altus E. "Tex," and Dorothy Nunley. Interview by Dennis McBride, June 9, 1986.

Parker, Robert. Interview by Dennis McBride, June 2 and November 9, 1986.

Pulsipher, Dean. Interview by Dennis McBride, August 19, 1986.

Wadman, Harold. Interview by Dennis McBride, December 21, 1986.

Young, Walker R. Interview by Elton Garrett and Teddy Fenton, June 23, 1975.

Ralph Roske Oral History Project on Early Las Vegas. Transcripts. Oral History Research Center. Special Collections and Archives. University Libraries, University of Nevada, Las Vegas.

Cahlan, John F. Interview by Lester Wisbrod, February 18, 1975.

Dieleman, Ruth, and Jake Dieleman. Interview by James M. Greene, November 15, 1974.

Emery, Murl. Interview by R. C. Turner, March 26 and April 2, 1976.

McCullough, William. Interview by Pete Wahlquist, February 26, 1979.

University of Nevada Oral History Program. Transcripts. University of Nevada, Reno.

Allen, Marion, Leo Dunbar, Erma Godbey, Carl Merrill, and Mary Ann Merrill. "Hoover Dam and Boulder City, 1931–1936: A Discussion Among Some Who Were There." Interview by R. T. King and Guy Rocha, September 17, 1985.

Godbey, Erma O. "Pioneering in Boulder City, Nevada." Interview by Mary Ellen Glass, March 7–9, 1966.

Merrill, Mary Ann. "Memories of Boulder City, 1932–1936." Interview by R. T. King, 1985.

PERIODICALS

Boulder City Journal, Boulder City, Nevada.

Imperial Valley Press, El Centro, California.

Las Vegas Age, Las Vegas, Nevada.

Las Vegas Evening Review-Journal, Las Vegas, Nevada.

Los Angeles Times, Los Angeles, California.

Reclamation Era, US Bureau of Reclamation, Washington, DC.

ARTICLES AND BOOKS

Allen, Marion V. *Hoover Dam & Boulder City.* Redding, CA: privately published, 1983.

Andrés, Benny J., Jr. *Power and Control in the Imperial Valley: Nature, Agribusiness, and Workers on the California Borderland, 1900–1940.* College Station: Texas A&M University Press, 2015.

Babcock & Wilcox Company. *Hoover Dam.* New York: Babcock & Wilcox, 1933.

Castle, Victor. "Well, I Quit My Job at the Dam." *Nation,* August 26, 1931, 207–8.

Compressed Air Magazine. The Story of the Hoover Dam. Reprint of twenty-three articles published 1931–1935. Las Vegas: Nevada Publications, 1986.

Dunar, Andrew J., and Dennis McBride. *Building Hoover Dam: An Oral History of the Great Depression.* Reno: University of Nevada Press, 1993.

Fitzgerald, Roosevelt. "Blacks and the Boulder Dam Project." *Nevada Historical Society Quarterly* 24, no. 3 (Fall 1981): 255–60.

Fortune. "The Dam." September 1933, 74–88.

Fortune. "The Earth Movers." Pts. 1, 2, and 3. August 1943, 99–107, 210–14; September 1943, 119–22, 219–26; October 1943, 139–44, 193–99.

Fradkin, Philip L. *A River No More: The Colorado River and the West.* Berkeley: University of California Press, 1995.

Harper, S. O., Walker R. Young, and W. V. Greeley. "Francis Trenholm Crowe, Hon. M. ASCE." Memoirs of Deceased Members. *Transactions of the American Society of Civil Engineers* 113 (1948): 1397–1403.

Hiltzik, Michael. *Colossus: The Turbulent, Thrilling Saga of the Building of Hoover Dam.* New York: Free Press, 2010.

Hundley, Norris, Jr. *Water and the West: The Colorado River Compact and the Politics of Water in the American West.* 2nd ed. Berkeley: University of California Press, 2009.

Kennan, George. *The Salton Sea: An Account of Harriman's Fight with the Colorado River.* New York: Macmillan, 1917.

Kennedy, David M. *Freedom from Fear: The American People in Depression and War, 1929–1945.* New York: Oxford University Press, 1999.

King, Judson. "Open Shop at Boulder Dam." *New Republic,* June 24, 1931, 147–48.

Kleinsorge, Paul L. *The Boulder Canyon Project: Historical and Economic Aspects.* Stanford, CA: Stanford University Press, 1941.

Kruman, Marc W. "Quotas for Blacks: The Public Works Administration and the Black Construction Worker." *Labor History* 16, no. 1 (Winter 1975): 37–51.

McBride, Dennis. *In the Beginning: A History of Boulder City, Nevada.* Boulder City, NV: Boulder City Chamber of Commerce, 1981.

Newell, F. H. "The Salton Sea." In *Annual Report of the Board of Regents of the Smithsonian Institution, 1907,* 331–45. Washington, DC: Government Printing Office, 1908.

Pettitt, George A. *So Boulder Dam Was Built.* Berkeley, CA: Lederer, Street & Zeus, 1935.

Reisner, Marc. *Cadillac Desert: The American West and Its Disappearing Water.* New York: Penguin Books, 1993.

Rocca, Al M. *America's Master Dam Builder: The Engineering Genius of Frank T. Crowe.* Lanham, MD: University Press of America, 2001.

Rocha, Guy Louis. "The IWW and the Boulder Canyon Project: The Final Death Throes of American Syndicalism." *Nevada Historical Society Quarterly* 21, no. 1 (Spring 1978): 3–24.

Six Companies, Inc. "Photographic Record, Hover Dam Project." 3 vols. September 1930 and May 1931–October 1935. Donated by H. J. Lawler. Utah Construction Company Hoover Dam Scrapbooks. Stewart Library, Weber State University, Ogden, Utah. cdm.weber.edu/digital/collection/HJLAW.

Stene, Eric A. *The All-American Canal System: Boulder Canyon Project.* Denver: Bureau of Reclamation, 1995.

Stevens, Joseph E. *Hoover Dam: An American Adventure.* Norman: University of Oklahoma Press, 1988.

Summitt, April R. *Contested Waters: An Environmental History of the Colorado River.* Boulder: University Press of Colorado, 2013.

US Bureau of Reclamation. "Annual Project History: Boulder Canyon Project Hoover Dam." https://catalog.archives.gov/id/2292774.

US Bureau of Reclamation. *Colorado River Basin Water Supply and Demand Study.* December 2012.

US Bureau of Reclamation. *The Story of Boulder Dam.* Conservation Bulletin No. 9. Washington, DC: Government Printing Office, 1941.

US National Park Service. *A Survey of the Recreational Resources of the Colorado River Basin.* Washington, DC: Government Printing Office, 1950.

US Reclamation Service. *Problems of the Imperial Valley and Vicinity.* Senate Doc. No. 142, 67th Congress. Washington, DC: Government Printing Office, 1922.

Vilander, Barbara. *Hoover Dam: The Photographs of Ben Glaha.* Tucson: University of Arizona Press, 1999.

Waters, Frank. *The Colorado.* The Rivers of America. New York: Rinehart, 1946.

Wilbur, Ray Lyman, and Elwood Mead. *The Construction of Hoover Dam: Preliminary Investigations, Design of Dam, and Progress of Construction.* Washington, DC: Government Printing Office, 1933.

Wilson, Edmund. "Hoover Dam." In *The American Earthquake: A Documentary of the Twenties and Thirties,* 368–78. New York: Farrar, Straus Giroux, 1979.

Wiltshire, Richard L., David R. Gilbert, and Jerry R. Rogers, eds. *Hoover Dam 75th Anniversary History Symposium.* Reston, VA: American Society of Civil Engineers, 2011.

Wolf, Donald E. *Big Dams and Other Dreams: The Six Companies Story.* Norman: University of Oklahoma Press, 1996.

Young, Walker R. "Mission of Boulder Dam Fulfilled." *Civil Engineering* 5, no. 6 (June 1935): 352–56.

Young, Walker R. "Significance of Boulder Canyon Project." *Civil Engineering* 5, no. 5 (May 1935): 279–83.

Zappia, Natale A. *Traders and Raiders: The Indigenous World of the Colorado Basin, 1540–1859.* Chapel Hill: University of North Carolina Press, 2014.

PHOTO CREDITS

Associated Press: 198

Bill Spengler/Alamy Stock Photo: 193

Bureau of Reclamation: xii, 10, 28, 80, 84, 86, 95, 100, 108, 110, 120, 121, 124, 126, 136, 141, 144, 156, 160, 166, 183

Bureau of Reclamation Photographs, UNLV Libraries Special Collections & Archives: 107, 117, 142, 146, 172, 192

Cline Library, Northern Arizona State University. Photograph by Tad Nichols: 187

Courtesy Metropolitan Water District of Southern California: 178

Courtesy of the author: 194

Courtesy of Special Collections Department, Stewart Library, Weber State University: 5, 70, 90, 91, 92, 96, 102, 105, 112, 115, 127, 132, 138, 164, 168

Dennis McBride Photograph Collection, UNLV Libraries Special Collections & Archives: 185

Dorothy Dorothy Photograph Collection, UNLV Libraries Special Collections & Archives: ii–iii

Elton and Madelaine Garrett Collection, UNLV Libraries Special Collections & Archives: 59, 66, 77

Henry J. Kaiser Pictorial Collection, The Bancroft Library, University of California, Berkeley: 75, 114 (BANC PIC 1983.001-.075)

James Cashman Sr. Photograph Collection, UNLV Libraries Special Collections & Archives: 159

James H. Down Jr. Photograph Collection, UNLV Libraries Special Collections & Archives: 3

Jim Broaddus/Aion Bookshop: 38, 39

KLVX Steamboats on the Colorado Collection, UNLV Libraries Special Collections & Archives: 154

L. F. Manis Photograph Collection, UNLV Libraries Special Collections & Archives: 152

Library of Congress: vi, viii, 25, 113, 174

Library Special Collections, Charles E. Young Research Library, UCLA: 14, 18, 19, 21, 43

Los Angeles Daily News Negatives, Library Special Collections, Charles E. Young Research Library, UCLA: 176

Los Angeles Times Photographic Archive, Library Special Collections, Charles E. Young Research Library, UCLA: 180

National Archives: x, 55

Nevada Mining Photograph Collection, UNLV Libraries Special Collections & Archives: 37 (bottom)

Pueblo Grande de Nevada Photograph Collection, UNLV Libraries Special Collections & Archives: 49

Ray Cutright Collection of Winthrop A. Davis Photographs, UNLV Libraries Special Collections & Archives: 37 (top), 62

Sierra Club, William E. Colby Memorial Library: 189

Southern California Edison Photographs and Negatives. Courtesy of the Huntington Library, San Marino, CA: 68

U.S. Geological Survey: 162

Union Pacific Railroad Photographs, UNLV Libraries Special Collections & Archives: 50, 52, 57, 60 (top), 60 (bottom), 61

Virginia "Teddy" Fenton Photograph Collection, UNLV Libraries Special Collections & Archives: 71, 130, 133, 158

Wisconsin Historical Society, WHI-86976: 8

INDEX

NOTE: *Italic page numbers* indicate photographs